Mathieu Dumas

Journal of a French Quartermaster on the March to Yorktown June 16—October 6, 1781

Translated and annotated by

Norman Desmarais

Revolutionary Imprints
Lincoln, Rhode Island

Copyright © 2022 by Norman Desmarais

All rights reserved.
No part of this publication may be reproduced, stored in a retrieval system, or transmitted, in any form or by any means, electronic, mechanical, photocopying, recording, or otherwise, without the prior written permission of the publisher.

ISBN: 978-0-578-29768-2

To my grandsons Lucas, Nathaniel and Thomas in hopes that they will benefit from my legacy and build on it.

Portrait of Mathieu Dumas (1753-1837) by Louise Adélaïde Desnos (1807-1870) commissioned by Louis Philippe for the museum of Versailles in 1842. Musee de l' Armée, Hotel National des Invalides, Paris.

Table of Contents

Illustrations vii
Acknowledgements ix
Introduction 1
   Mathieu Dumas 4
      The Campaign in America (1780-1783) 6
      The Last Years of the Ancien Régime and the Revolution 9
      The Empire and the Restoration 11
      From Louis XVIII to the Revolution of 1830 13
   History of This Diary 14
   The Historical Significance of the Draft
   for the Campaign Journal 16
   Comparison with the Description of his American
   Stay in his Memoirs 17
   Translator Notes 19
1781 23
June 23
July 37
August 61
September 85
October 119

Appendix 1 123

Reconnaissance of the positions at Portsmouth and of the British works in this part of Virginia. 123

Article 1 Exterior Reconnaissance 124

Article 2 Interior Reconnaissance 127

Measurements of the British Works at Portsmouth 128

Appendix 2 131

Travels in Virginia in 1782 131

Observations on Porto Cabello 138

Voyage to Carragne 140

Sources and Bibliography 143

Archives 143

Bibliography 144

Index 153

About the Editor 159

Illustrations

Cover: detail of Querenet De La Combe. Siege d'York, 1781. Plan d'York en Virginie avec les attaques et les campemens de l'Armée combinée de France et d'Amérique. Library of Congress. Scale ca. 1:14,640.

Frontispiece. Portrait of Mathieu Dumas iv
Fig. 1. Grenadier of the Bourbonnais Regiment 34
Fig. 2. Régiment Saintonge 36
Fig. 3. Reproduction of the French frigate *Hermione* 47
Fig. 4. A hussar of the Estherazy Regiment 52
Fig. 5. French siege artillery at Yorktown 60
Fig. 6. French camp at Phillipsburg 70
Fig. 7. Artillery on carriages with caissons 78
Fig. 8. Uniforms of the Royal Deux-Ponts Regiment 80
Fig. 9. Zebulon Hollingsworth's house 86
Fig. 10. The French camp site at Scott's Plantation 102
Fig. 11. Joanna Lloyd and Richard Bennett Lloyd 104
Fig. 12. French howitzer and a 13-inch mortar 114
Fig. 13. Communication trench 116
Fig. 14. Gabions and fascines 120

Acknowledgements

My wife Barbara deserves an immense debt of gratitude for her support and encouragement and for everything she does to allow me the freedom to pursue my research and writing.

Mathieu Dumas's penmanship is very difficult to read. One can go bug-eyed very quickly. Bertrand Van Ruymbeke and Iris de Rode saved me many hours of very difficult reading by transcribing the manuscript. Their work was published under the title *La Marche sur Yorktown: Le Journal de Mathieu Dumas (16 juin —6 octobre, 1781)*. Images of the manuscript appear on the even pages and the transcription on the facing odd pages. This makes it quite easy to compare the two and to locate particular passages.

The French version has no annotations whereas this translation identifies the people and places which are often misspelled and nearly incomprehensible in the manuscript.

I also thank my good friend and fellow researcher Dr. Robert Selig. Bob is undoubtedly the most knowledgeable person alive about the Washington-Rochambeau trail. In fact, his name is synonymous with it as he was, and continues to be, the historian for the trail. Bob brought this diary to my attention and has been my consultant and a sounding board throughout the translation process. He proofread the many drafts and provided information and guidance for many of the footnotes. I am deeply grateful and I treasure our friendship.

Introduction

Most diaries of the American War of Independence era were written toward the end of the author's life. Some may have been spurred on by pension applications, 50 years after the war began. Many were written so the author could transmit to his children and grandchildren his accounts of what he did during the war.

Mathieu Dumas is no exception. He completed his *Souvenirs Du Lieutenant-Général Cte Mathieu Dumas, de 1770 À 1836* during the last year of his life. He dedicated it to his son Christian who had it published in three volumes two years later in 1839[1]. Excerpts were translated into English the same year and published in two volumes under the title *Memoirs of his Own Time; Including the Revolution, the Empire, and the Restoration.*

Most of the soldiers probably recorded their thoughts in their free time and edited and transcribed them into a more formal manuscript later. Very few of these notes still survive. *La Marche sur Yorktown: Le Journal de Mathieu Dumas (16 juin —6 octobre, 1781)* transcribed by Bertrand Van Ruymbeke and Iris de Rode is one of the few that remain.

The Quartermaster General of the Army, Pierre François de Béville (1721-1798), had five aides Alexandre-Théodore-Victor, comte de Lameth (1760-1829), Jacques Anne Joseph le Prestre, comte de Vauban (1754-1815), Hans Axel, comte de Fersen

---

[1] Dumas, Mathieu. Souvenirs Du Lieutenant-Général Cte Mathieu Dumas, de 1770 À 1836. C. Gosselin, 1839. Excerpts were translated into English as Memoirs of his Own Time; Including the Revolution, the Empire, and the Restoration. By Lieut.-Gen. Count Mathieu Dumas. London: Richard Bentley, 1839.

(1755-1810), Louis François Bertrand Dupont d'Aubevoye, comte de Lauberdière (1759-1837) and Mathieu Dumas (1753-1837). Louis Alexandre Berthier was also attached to the corps of quartermasters but most of his job was mapping the camps.

It does not appear that Béville or Vauban kept diaries. Lameth's memoirs[2] say very little about his time in America. There is a brief (4 pages) section on the siege and surrender of Yorktown that offers nothing new to our knowledge of those events. The Comte de Fersen's journal[3] contains a series of letters to his father during the American campaigns. He wrote frequently during the garrison period. His last letter before the march to Yorktown is dated June 3, 1781. His next letter, dated October 23, 1781, apologizes for not writing sooner because he "had no time to write you the slightest detail" (p.47). He then includes a "Journal of Operations during the Siege and Surrender of Yorktown" (5 ½ pages) and another letter of the same date (1 ½ pages) that give a brief account of the major events of the previous three and a half months.

Louis François Bertrand Dupont d'Aubevoye, comte de Lauberdière[4], Louis Alexandre Berthier and Mathieu Dumas are the only French assistant quartermasters general to have kept any account of their work and travels during the march.

Besides being one of three extant diaries by a French quartermaster, this diary is unique because it focuses on the author's daily business, as he states: "This book will be filled with my business and my thoughts." So we get a glimpse of the day-to-day activities of an assistant quartermaster and his thoughts and impressions recorded contemporaneously and unedited. The two diaries also give us

---

2 Lameth, Alexandre, and Welvert Eugène. Mémoires. Fontemoing, 1913.

3 Fersen, Hans Axel von. *Diary and Correspondence of Count Axel Fersen*. Hardy, Pratt, 1902.

4 The Count de Lauberdière's diary is at the Bibliothèque Nationale and available at: http://gallica.bnf.fr/ark:/12148/btv1b52506900t/f17.image. It was translated into English: Lauberdière Louis François Bertrand Dupont d'Aubevoye. *The Road to Yorktown: The French Campaigns in the American Revolution, 1780-1783*. Edited by Norman Desmarais, Savas Beatie, 2020.

much information about the logistics of supplying and supporting the French army overseas.

The quartermasters were staff officers who were responsible for the procurement and distribution of food, clothing and supplies as well as for reconnoitering travel routes, the repair and maintenance of roads and bridges; the layout, organization and construction of camps; the supply and maintenance of wagons and teams and of boats for water transport[5].

Moreover, Dumas took a different route to cross the Susquehanna River than did Lauberdière and half of the army. After leaving Head of Elk (Elkton, Maryland), the left column crossed the Susquehanna River at Lower Ferry (now known as Havre de Grace, Maryland). The right column, composed of all of Lauzun's hussars, the artillery and the baggage crossed at the ford of Bald Friar's Ferry. This added a day's march (about 20 miles) to the voyage and the crossing presented many difficulties. Dumas was surprised that there were no serious accidents that occurred that would delay them from rejoining the left column at Bushtown (Harford, Maryland). He provides all the details in his text. Moreover, Dumas was in the fortunate group that boarded ships at Annapolis to go to Williamsburg, Virginia prior to marching to Yorktown.

Dumas was an impressionable 27-year-old when he came to America. He wrote his *Souvenirs* 56 years later at the age of 83. While he probably consulted this draft when writing his *Souvenirs*, the volumes make very little, if any, reference to his work as a quartermaster. Comparing the draft with the published journal, one can appreciate how the author's viewpoint changed over the years. It is also interesting to compare the two documents to determine what this man considered important at various stages of his life, what was omitted and what was changed.

In order to facilitate such a study, this translation retains as much of the crossed out text as possible. Some words or passages

---

5 Risch, Erna, and Center of Military History. *Supplying Washington's Army*. Center of Military History, United States Army, 1981. Huston, James A. *The Sinews of War : Army Logistics, 1775-1953*. Office of the Chief of Military History, United States Army, 1966.

are too obliterated to reconstruct or are illegible. The sentences read coherently without the strikeouts, but it is sometimes interesting to notice how the author changes his mind or uses different words.

Young Dumas was particularly impressed with the natural beauty of America, particularly the trees. Later, like all the French diarists, he turns his attention to the women:

> Before leaving Baltimore, a brief word about the women as I speak constantly about the trees. They are generally not pretty. This evening, I saw a rather large gathering at Mr. Smith's and there were only one or two people of note. They comported themselves ridiculously. They seemed flirtatious and unpleasant to me.

He talks about his injury when his horse fell on him:

> I made great haste and arrived at North Salem at nightfall. I expected to get a relay there as my horse faltered and I fell underneath, still in the saddle. My foot was so badly trampled before I was able to disengage myself that it was impossible to mount a horse. I arrived at the first house with difficulty.

He continues to describe how he performed his work until he recovered.

We now turn our attention to the author.

Mathieu Dumas

Mathieu Dumas (1753-1837) had a great military and administrative career, extending through the reign of Louis XVI, the Revolution, the Consulate and the Empire, the Restoration under Louis XVIII and Charles X, and finally the Revolution of 1830. He is practically unknown today. It is possible to reconstruct his life from his own *memoirs* that he wrote to his son just before his death, archival material relating to his military career, and a biographical sketch published in 1842 and another in 2005[6]. Kenneth A. Duncan compiled a biography (*Mathieu Dumas: a biography*) as his doctoral thesis at the University of St Andrews in 1974.

Mathieu Dumas was born in Montpellier on November 23, 1753. His parents were Mathieu Dumas (1710- ?), Treasurer of France, and Anne de Loÿs (dates unknown), who belonged to a family of the judiciary. He was educated by his uncle, canon and grand archdeacon of the diocesan Chapter in Montpellier for an ecclesiastical career. However, at the age of 13, Dumas decided against the priesthood and prepared for a military career. He went to Paris to study mathematics, hoping to be admitted to l'École d'Application de Génie (the School of Applied Engineering). He became a candidate for the first class but was not selected. He entered the army directly in the Médoc infantry regiment as a chasseur (light infantryman) with a commission as second lieutenant. Mathieu's two brothers, Guillaume Mathieu Dumas de St Marcel (1755-1826) and Dumas de St. Fulcran (dates unknown), also pursued a military career. The Dumas brothers crossed paths during various military campaigns[7].

Mathieu Dumas learned to conduct military reconnaissance as well as to draw maps in the Alps during his first years in the army.

---

6   Archives Nationales, symbol LH/843/35, dossier Comte Dumas, « Dumas Military State »Online: http://www2.culture.gouv.fr/public/mistral/leonore_fr?ACTION=CHERCHER &FIELD_1=COTE&VALUE_1=LH/843/35. Wahlen, Auguste. *Nouveau Dictionnaire de la Conversation; Ou, Répertoire Universel ... Sur Le Plan Du Conversation's Lexicon ... Par Une Société De Littérateurs, de Savants et D'Artistes.* Librairie-Historique-Artistique, 1842. Bodinier, Gilbert, et al. *Dictionnaire Des Officiers de L'Armée Royale Qui Ont Combattu Aux Etats-Unis Pendant la Guerre d'Indépendance, 1776-1783: Suivi D'un Supplément À Les Français Sous Les Treize Étoiles Du Commandant André Lasseray.* 4e éd. augm. et corr ed., Service Historique de l'Armée de Terre, 2005. Dumas, Mathieu. *Souvenirs Du Lieutenant-Général Cte Mathieu Dumas, de 1770 À 1836.* C. Gosselin, 1839 (3 vols.). Excerpts were translated into *Memoirs of his Own Time; Including the Revolution, the Empire, and the Restoration.* By. Lieut.-Gen. Count Mathieu Dumas. London: Richard Bentley, 1839. (2 vols.) As the French version is more detailed, we will cite from the French version in the following references.

7   Guillaume Mathieu Dumas de St Marcel is the brother he meets in his diary.

However, he never became a geographer engineer, the official function of cartographer in the army. Yet, his talents will still be called upon for this task several times in his career.

When Dumas learned about the American War of Independence in 1775, he wanted to go to America with Marie Jean Paul Joseph du Motier Marquis de Lafayette (1757-1834) to help the Thirteen Colonies and to advance his career. His desire proved fruitless at this time. The Comte de Puységur[8], inspector general of the infantry, noticed him and appointed him as aide-de-camp in 1777. The following year, Puységur recommended Dumas to General Rochambeau. Rochambeau had been appointed general of the French army after the signing of the Franco-American alliance. Dumas became his aide-de-camp. He was promoted to captain in 1779, in preparation for an invasion of England. Dumas reconnoitered the ports to prepare for this invasion which never occurred[9].

As Rochambeau's aide-de-camp, Dumas arrived in America on July 17, 1780 with the French expeditionary force. He was twenty-seven years old and he stayed there for a period of about two years. While crossing the Atlantic, Dumas thought the fleet was sailing to Saint Domingue[10], but they arrived in Newport, Rhode Island after a long sea voyage of 71 days[11].

The Campaign in America (1780-1783)

Pierre François de Béville (1721-1798) was Quartermaster General of the Army and Dumas was one of his aides. In that capacity, Dumas was responsible for providing for all the needs of the small army's camp. He helped with the preparations, but he was mainly responsible for reconnoitering and drawing maps of the region in

---

8 François Jacques Chastenet, Marquis de Puységur (1716-1782). Dumas served as his aide-de-camp in 1777.
9 Archives Nationales, LH/843/35, Dossier Comte Dumas, « Etat Militaire Dumas ».
10 Now Haiti.
11 He describes the crossing in great detail in his *Souvenirs*. Vol. 1 pp. 30-40.

order to provide the necessary information for the preparation of the next campaign[12]. Dumas was not a professional cartographer and Louis Alexandre Berthier (1753-1815), Rochambeau's aide-de-camp and cartographer, had not yet arrived. General Rochambeau called upon "drawing cadets or officers," such as Mathieu Dumas, and Baron von Closen, of the Royal Deux-Ponts regiment.

Dumas later wrote essays "on topography," and "on the service of the general staffs," on the development of the creation of maps and on the role of topographical engineers in the preparation of campaigns. Dumas was also in charge of transmitting Rochambeau's letters to General George Washington (1732–1799), a great honor. He later wrote about it: "I have received from him a paternal welcome." He and Washington, accompanied by Lafayette, also made reconnaissance together[13]. Dumas remained mainly in Providence, Rhode Island with a Dr. Brown during the winter of 1780-1781. He learned the English language and American customs there[14].

At the end of the winter, the new campaign had to be prepared, and, following the Wethersfield Conference, the French army set out to join the Continental Army near New York. Dumas assisted Quartermaster General de Béville in organizing marches and camps, and in gathering geographical information for the army. Béville's other aides were Alexandre-Théodore-Victor, comte de Lameth (1760-1829), Jacques Anne Joseph le Prestre, comte de Vauban (1754-1815), Hans Axel von, Comte de Fersen (1755-1810), and Louis François Bertrand Dupont d'Aubevoye, comte de Lauberdière. Dumas and his friend and faithful companion de Lameth oversaw the crossing of the Hudson, Delaware, and Susquehanna rivers[15]. This book deals with this march.

After the march and the siege of Yorktown, the French army again entered winter camp, the details of which Dumas prepared.

---

12 One example of a Dumas map was printed in H.C. Rice, Anna S.K Brown. *The American Campaigns of Rochambeau's Army*, vol. 2, p.125.
13 Dumas. *Souvenirs*. Vol. 1 p. 53.
14 Ibid., p. 43.
15 Wahlen op. cit. p.370.

He continued to make reconnaissances during this winter period, even though there was no definite plan for a new campaign for the summer of 1782. He also had time to travel. He visited several former battlefields to analyze the battles on location and stayed a few weeks in Boston. He also visited an establishment of the Moravian Brothers which he found very interesting for their egalitarian ideas[16].

Part of the army left for France with General Rochambeau in January 1783. Another division left to campaign in Jamaica to protect the lucrative sugar islands. Dumas was then the oldest assistant quartermaster general. He became head of the general staff of the army corps under the orders of General de Vioménil[17] and became part of the expedition to Jamaica[18].

During the journey to the islands, Dumas wrote his observations on the situation in the United States. He compared the national character of the Americans with that of the British, described the disastrous effect of the war on the various states, made observations on the political and commercial future of the United States and ended with a long description of all thirteen American states. Some of the same observations appear in some passages of this diary[19].

Dumas arrived at the tip of Puerto Rico on January 15, 1783 to await the arrival of the French fleet. He made an excursion, at that time, with the Count of Ségur, the Prince of Broglie and Berthier to discover the surroundings. Eventually, the campaign in Jamaica did not take place, as peace was signed on September 3, 1783. England recognized American independence. As soon as they received this news, Dumas went to Saint Domingue, to prepare the return of the army to France. Traveling through this island, he is very touched by "the horrors of slavery" and its "market of the underworld". Dumas returned to France in the winter of 1783[20].

---

16 Dumas, *Souvenirs*, Vol.1, pp. 93-94.
17 Antoine Charles du Houx baron de Vioménil (1728-1792)
18 Archives Nationales, LH/843/35, « Dossier Comte Dumas», « Etat Militaire Dumas », see also Dumas, Souvenirs. Vol. 1, pp.15-163.
19 Dumas, *Souvenirs*, vol. 1, pp.112-130.
20 Ibid. pp. 158-159.

The Last Years of the Ancien Régime and the Revolution

Upon his return to France, Dumas was promoted to the rank of major at the age of twenty-nine. He was sent to reconnoiter the Cyclades Archipelago and the island of Candia (Crete) in 1784. He was then sent to Turkey and the surrounding areas in 1786 to inspect the status of the military in the eastern Mediterranean[21]. He was promoted to colonel when he returned to France and became a member of the Society of the Cincinnati[22].

Dumas married Marie Adelaïde Julie Delarue (1770-1807) on February 17, 1785. They had three children, including two daughters, Cornélie (1786-1856) and Octavie (1788), who died in infancy, and a son, Christian Léon (1789-1873), who became a general and published his father's memoirs. The couple divorced in 1801[23].

Dumas was sent to Amsterdam in 1787 to defend the city against the Prussians during the Patriot Revolution of 1785–1787[24]. He received the cross of Saint Louis that year, and, the following year, he replaced General Guibert as secretary of Louis XVI's War Council and was employed in various missions, particularly in Alsace[25].

The "first troubles in Paris" began in 1789 when Dumas was thirty-six years old[26]. He organized the National Guards with Lafayette at the beginning of the Revolution, and he was appointed quartermaster general of the army. The king sent him to Rouen and then to the south of France to pacify the lands[27]. He was later appointed the king's commissioner in Alsace with civil and military

---

21 Archives Nationales, LH/843/35: « Dossier Comte Dumas », « Etat Militaire Dumas » and correspondence. See also Dumas, *Souvenirs*, vol. 1 book/chapter 3.
22 See Ludovic de Contenson, *La société de Cincinnati de France et la guerre d'Amérique 1778-1783*. Paris, Editions Picard, première édition 1913, nouvelle édition 2016, and https://www.cincinnatidefrance.fr/
23 Wahlen. *Nouveau dictionnaire de la Conversation,* 372. This was possible because of new laws passed during the French Revolution legalizing divorce.
24 Archives Nationales, LH/843/35, « Dossier Comte Dumas »; « Revolution Anti Stadthouderienne »
25 Dumas. *Souvenirs* books 3 and 4.
26 Ibid. vol. 1 p. 428.
27 Wahlen. op. cit., p. 371.

powers. He returned to Paris in 1791 to the military committee of the Constitutional Convention. As commander of the National Guard, he brought Louis XVI back to Paris after his arrest in Varennes[28]. He was promoted to major general and governor of Metz and director of the war depot the same year. There he organized the first mounted artillery company in France[29].

On his return from Metz, he was elected to the Legislative Assembly as Deputy of Seine et Oise. During the French Revolution, he tried above all to maintain peace and order, especially during the Reign of Terror. He opposed the declaration of war against Austria[30] and served as a member of the Council of Five Hundred in 1792[31]. Revolutionaries stormed the Tuileries on August 10, 1792 and Dumas was threatened enough that he had to hide. He left France in disguise and went to Switzerland. He was accused of having given campaign plans to the enemies[32]. He managed to escape to England but returned to Paris a few weeks later to get his wife and children. They moved to Switzerland in September[33]. After the Thermidorian Reaction brought down Robespierre and the situation became safer, Dumas returned to Paris in 1795 and entered the Council of Elders, fighting against anarchy and supporting, along with the minority of the Directory, the system of peace and moderation that was beginning to regain favor in the country[34].

But the coup d'état of 18 Fructidor (4 September 1797) put an end to these plans. Dumas had to flee again because of his moderate

---

28 Ibid.
29 Archives Nationales LH/843/35, « Dossier Comte Dumas », « État Militaire Dumas ».
30 Dumas. *Souvenirs*, t. 1., p. 432
31 Wahlen op. cit., p. 372. Council of Five Hundred (Conseil de Cinq-Cents) was the lower house of the legislative body established by France's Constitution of 1795 (Year III of the French Revolution). It consisted of 500 delegates and initiated legislation, which the upper house, the Council of Ancients, accepted or rejected. It also provided the upper house with a list of candidates from which the five members of the Directory, the executive branch, were to be chosen. The council governed from 1795 to 1799 (the period known as the Directory). It was dissolved in a coup that effectively ended the French Revolution.
32 Archives Nationales LH/843/35, « Dossier Comte Dumas », « État Militaire Dumas ».
33 Wahlen. op. cit., p. 372.
34 *Ibid.*

views. He first tried to return to America, as evidenced by his correspondence with his American friends, George Washington and Alexander Hamilton[35]. This trip was too complicated to organize so he went to Hamburg, Germany, where he began to write the first chapters of his book *Précis des Événements Militaires*[36].

The Empire and the Restoration

After 18 Brumaire (November 9, 1799), Napoléon Bonaparte (1769-1821) came to power and recalled Dumas to Paris in 1801 to be reintegrated into the army as a brigadier general at the age of forty-eight[37]. He was sent to Dijon to organize the Army of the Reserve and to serve as chief of staff under the command of General Guillaume Marie-Anne Brune[38]. After completing this mission, he was placed at the head of the general staff of the Army of the Grisons, under the command of General Etienne-Jacques-Joseph- Alexandre McDonald[39]. He served as an intermediary between this army and the Army of Italy during the famous crossing of the Splugen glaciers (Italo-Swiss border, November 1800)[40].

He was recalled to the war section of the Council of State in 1802 at the time when Napoleon created the Legion of Honor. He

---

35 Mathieu Dumas to George Washington (24 January 1789), founders.archives. gov/documents/Washington/99-01-02-00214 not to be confused with his brother's (Guillaume Mathieu Dumas) correspondence with Washington. Founders.archives.gov/documents/Washington/06-01-02-0167, and Dumas to Hamilton, (8 December 1797). Founders.archives.gov/documents/Hamilton/01-21-02-0179. Lafayette also wrote a letter to Hamilton about Dumas (December 8, 1797), founders.archives.gov/documents/Hamilton/01-21-02-0180.
36 Dumas, Mathieu, and Ambroise Tardieu. *Précis Des Évènemens Militaires, Ou Essais Historiques Sur Les Campagnes de 1799 À 1814: Avec Cartes Et Plans*. Chez Treuttel Et Würtz, 1816.
37 Archives Nationales, LH/843/35, « Dossier Comte Dumas », « État Militaire Dumas ».
38 Guillaume Marie-Anne Brune, 1st Count Brune (1764 –1815)
39 Étienne Jacques-Joseph-Alexandre Macdonald, 1st Duke of Taranto (1765 –1840.
40 Archives Nationales, LH/843/35, « Dossier Comte Dumas », « État Militaire Dumas ». 46.505556, 9.330278.

appointed Dumas to the commission responsible for preparing the legislation.

Dumas rose in the military hierarchy of the Grande Armée. He was appointed successively: commander at the camp at Boulogne, major general, assistant major general and quartermaster general. He participated in the Battle of Austerlitz (December 2, 1805), and in the Dalmatian campaigns (1806-1807). He was appointed Minister of War of Naples under King Joseph Bonaparte[41] in 1803, then Grand Marshal of Naples[42]. He then went to Spain, where Napoleon appointed him major general in the Army of Spain. After various duties there, Dumas was sent back to France to prepare a campaign across the Rhine, where he was in charge of inspecting the fortifications and magazines of all the corps. He participated in the Battle of Wagram in Austria on July 5 and 6, 1809. Dumas then went to Vienna to organize the evacuation of the French from the Austrian provinces. After all his campaigns, it was time for rewards: Napoleon named him Grand Officer of the Legion of Honor and he received other decorations from several monarchs of the empire[43].

During the peace interval (1810-1812), marked by Napoleon's second marriage and the birth of the future King of Rome, Dumas received the title of Count of the Empire in 1810 and resumed his work as director general of arsenals and conscription at the Council of State.

Napoléon had more and more confidence in him and appointed him Comptroller General of the Grande Armée for the Russian campaign in 1812. During this disastrous campaign, Dumas was captured and imprisoned in Hungary in 1813, after the Battle of Leipzig (October 16-19, 1813)[44].

---

41 Joseph of Naples 1st king 1806-1808.
42 Wahlen. op. cit., p. 373.
43 *Ibid.*
44 see Dumas. *Souvenirs*. Vol. 3 books 9-17.

From Louis XVIII to the Revolution of 1830

Dumas returned from captivity in 1814 at the age of sixty-one. He allied himself with the new king, Louis XVIII, who appointed him a member of a commission responsible for verifying the titles and claims of former émigré officers. The king then sent him to arrest Napoleon during his march back from the island of Elba but to no avail. Dumas resumed his old titles and others during the "Hundred Days."

When Louis XVIII returned to the throne after Napoleon's defeat at Waterloo, he sent Dumas into retirement for supporting Napoleon. Dumas took advantage of this period to resume writing his *Précis des Événements Militaires*[45].

Louis XVIII recalled Dumas two years later and reinstated him as president of the war committee in the Council of State, as a member of the committee for the defense of the kingdom and the government commissioner to support the war budget in both chambers. During this time, he finalized his 19-volume work, including the narration of the campaigns of 1799 and 1800-1807. He followed up on this work several years later, publishing and annotating the translation of the English work of the author William Napier (1785-1860), History of the War in the Peninsula[46].

Dumas retired from the army in September 1815, but he resumed a military career in 1818. After the death of Louis XVIII, Dumas did not support the new monarch, Charles X. Dumas, who was now seventy-five years old and a candidate in the electoral college of the first arrondissement of Paris, voted the Address of the 221[47] in the elections of 1828. He supported the cause of the Revolution

---

45 Wahlen. Op. cit., p.375.
46 Napier, William Francis Patrick. *History of the War in the Peninsula*. D. Christy, 1836 translated as *Histoire de la Guerre Dans la Peninsule et Dans le Midi de la France Depuis 1807 Jusqu'à 1814*. T. 2, Treuttel & Würtz, 1828.
47 The Address of the 221 was an address to King Charles X of France by the chamber of deputies at the opening of the French parliament on March 18, 1830. It expressed the defiance of the chamber's liberal majority of 221 deputies to the ministry headed by Jules, prince de Polignac, and helped lead to the July Revolution.

of 1830[48] and he "must be counted among those who contributed the most to cementing it[49]." As in 1789, his former friend General Lafayette called upon him to help reorganize the citizen militia[50].

Dumas was appointed inspector general of the kingdom's National Guards in 1830, although he had become virtually blind. During the reorganization of these troops, he resigned from this position in order to become vice-president of war and the navy. After his re-election to the Chamber of Deputies in 1831, he was made a Peer of France. He died six years later, on October 17, 1837, at the age of eighty-four, just after finalizing his *Souvenirs*, addressed to his son, who published them in 1839. Dumas left to posterity a reputation as a skillful general, a conscientious legislator and a distinguished writer.

History of This Diary

Mathieu Dumas wrote his notes, thoughts and impressions, which are the subject of this volume, between June and October 1781. His *Souvenirs* tells us the rest of the story of this diary:

> I had left at Providence, in the house of Dr. Bowen, and especially intrusted to his amiable daughters, a small box containing various papers and the notes which I had made in the course of our two campaigns. This box, which I supposed to be lost, has been carefully preserved by Mrs. Ward, the youngest of those ladies, the only survivor of her family, and who has done me the honour to remember me. After a lapse of forty years, having met at New York with General La Fayette during his triumphal progress, Mrs. Ward was so good as to enquire after me,

---

48 Caron, Jean-Claude. *La France De 1815 À 1848*. Troisième édition. Armand Colin, 2013.
49 Wahlen. op. cit., p. 375.
50 Ibid. Dumas. *Souvenirs*. Vol.1 p. 442.

and requested the general to convey this box to me, with an affecting testimony of our former, friendship. The notes, which I have thus recovered, have served me to make the sketch which I have inserted above[51].

After being used to write Dumas's *Souvenirs*, the contents of the little box were dispersed. One of the documents, this diary, traveled through France, only to be found in Sainte-Foy-la-Grande in 2015 by Dominique Mignon, the president of the Society for the History of Protestantism in the Dordogne Valley. She received a briefcase containing documents belonging to a family of the region. One of those documents was this diary. The rest of the contents of Dumas's box have not (yet) been found[52]...

Dumas's diary covers the period from June 16 to October 5, 1781, during which the French army made two marches: first to New York (June 18 to July 6) and second to Yorktown, Virginia together with the Continental Army (August 18 to September 28) after a stay

---

51 Dumas, Mathieu. *Souvenirs Du Lieutenant-Général Cte Mathieu Dumas, De 1770 À 1836*. C. Gosselin, 1839. Vol. 1 p. 159; Extracts were translated into English as *Memoirs of his own Time; Including the Revolution, the Empire, and the Restoration*. By Lieut.-Gen. Count Mathieu Dumas. London: Richard Bentley, 1839. Vol. 1 p. 113. The "two campaigns" refer to the American War of Independence and the second one in Jamaica. Congress invited Marquis Gilbert du Motier de Lafayette (1754-1834) to the United States in 1825 and 1826 to celebrate the 50th anniversary of the American War of Independence and his role in it. For more about this voyage, see Brandon, Edgar Ewing, editor. *A Pilgrimage of Liberty: A Contemporary Account of the Triumphal Tour of General Lafayette through the Southern and Western States in 1825, As Reported by the Local Newspapers*. Athens, Ohio: Lawhead Press, 1944. And the account of Lafayette's personal secretary Auguste Levasseur. *Lafayette En Amérique, En 1824 et 1825, Ou, Journal D'un Voyage Aux États-Unis*. Baudouin, 1829 translated into English by Alan R Hoffman: Levasseur, Auguste, and Alan R Hoffman. *Lafayette in America, in 1824 and 1825: Journal of a Voyage to the United States*. 1st ed., Lafayette Press, 2006.

52 The *Draft* does not indicate an author's name, but he can be determined with certainty to be Mathieu Dumas. Throughout the text, it is clear that the author is an assistant quartermaster general under the command of Pierre François de Béville (1721-1798), quartermaster general of the French army in America during the year 1781. The author mentions a multitude of people throughout his draft who can be Identified. He also writes several times about his brother, Dumas de St Marcel (1755-1826), who is in America at the same time.

at Philipsburg (from July 6 to August 18). This march crossed nine states covering a total of about 640 miles (950 kilometers)[53]. The diary also describes the beginning of the siege of Yorktown which lasted from September 28 until October 15 1781.

The Historical Significance of the Draft for the Campaign Journal

What is the historical significance of Dumas's draft? Documents similar to those of Dumas's draft have been published. Howard Rice lists about 100 journals reporting on the campaign and the people Dumas knew including: Baron von Closen, Louis-Alexandre Berthier, Axel von Fersen, the Chevalier de Chastellux[54].

The military information in these newspapers is very similar to that in Dumas's diary, such as the geographical details of the march and the problems they encountered en route. Dumas's text illustrates perfectly the concerns of the French army of that time, with the details of the circumstances of the campaign and the intervention of the various officials in the organization of the movement of the army between Providence, Rhode Island and Yorktown, Virginia, as well as the practical difficulties to be solved. These military details can shed light or historical knowledge on unknown details in the

---

53   Selig, Robert. *March to Victory: Washington, Rochambeau, and the Yorktown Campaign of 1781.* Center of Military History, 2005. p.3.
54   For a complete list, see Rice, Howard C, et al. *The American Campaigns of Rochambeau's Army, 1780, 1781, 1782, 1783.* Princeton University Press, 1972. Volume 1. Closen, Ludwig, et al. *The Revolutionary Journal of Baron Ludwig Von Closen, 1780-1783.* Published for the Institute of Early American History and Culture at Williamsburg, Va. by the University of North Carolina Press, 1958. Louis-Alexandre Berthier, *Diary of the Americas Campaign* (10 May 1780-26 August 1781. Fersen, Hans Axel von, and Fredrik Axel von Fersen. Lettres d'Axel de Fersen À Son Père: Pendant la Guerre de l'Indépendance d'Amérique. Edited by F. U Wrangel, Firmin-Didot et Cie, 1929. Chastellux, François-Jean de, et al. *Voyages de M. le Marquis De Chastellux Dans l'Amérique Septentrionale, Dans les Années 1780, 1781 & 1782.* Seconde édition ed., Chez Prault, Imprimeur Du Roi, 1788); Chastellux François Jean. Travels in North-America [in the Years 1780, 1781, and 1782. New York Times, 1968.

field, logistics and the functioning of communication between the different units of the army.

What is more particular to the draft is the very detailed day-to-day description. Most of the other logs were rewritten afterward, with drafts often lost. Dumas's draft also includes non-military reflections that make the draft particularly alive. These demonstrate his concerns, his interest in the country and its development. He wrote several times about the inhabitants (women in particular) of the different states, trade, the effects of war on the economy and on agriculture. He often wrote about the natural beauty of America. These kinds of reflections are interesting because they are quite rare in military writings, and they represent the thoughts of a Frenchman of the late eighteenth century on America.

Comparison with the Description of his American Stay in his Memoirs

Dumas's *Souvenirs* includes a chapter of about 140 pages that deals with the campaign in America from the preparations at Brest in 1780 until the return to the same port in 1783. Comparing the *Souvenirs* and the draft, we note several differences.

First, the draft describes two and a half months of the expedition in 77 pages while the *Souvenirs* devote only 12 pages to the same period. Dumas mentions[55] that he used his draft to write his *Souvenirs* after receiving it from Lafayette, but this does not appear explicitly in his text. The draft ends on October 5, 1781, in the midst of the Siege of Yorktown, which would last until October 19. One can imagine that he did not have time to write during the siege and that the draft ends suddenly for this reason. Dumas also does not

---

55 That passage begins on June 18 and the paragraphs are entitled « départ de l'armée française, marche de l'armée française, réunion de deux armées, position des armées, reconnaissances, disposition de Lord Cornwallis, passage de l'Hudson, arrivée à Philadelphie, Combat entre les escadres, passage de Susquehana, réunion de l'armée, le siège de Yorktown. Dumas, *Souvenirs*. vol. 1, pp. 67-79.

finish his own description of this period in his *Souvenirs*. He wrote until September 26, and then he quoted Rochambeau's journal to describe the Siege of Yorktown: "In tracing the memories of this glorious campaign, I have before my eyes rochambeau's excellent memoirs[56]."

Second, the nature of the text. The draft was written quickly, day by day, during the march. As a result, it is very anecdotal and contains a lot of specific details. The *Souvenirs* were written more than fifty years later. The passage covering the period of June to October is integrated into a detailed description of Dumas's life and its context. The few pages in the *Souvenirs* that describe the period covered by the diary rather form an analysis of the context of the American campaign. This passage contains very little information about Dumas himself. He wrote about his own role in the march and the Siege of Yorktown only twice. This difference in the nature of the two texts results in an opposition between anecdotes and analysis. His *Souvenirs* briefly describes the army's march and plans and preparations for the Siege of Yorktown. The diary describes in great detail all the preparations that Dumas was taking, as well as the complications of this mission.

Many of the details in the diary are not in his *Souvenirs*: the places where he is every day, his occupations, the people he meets, his ideas about the American people and the country. Other more negative information about the march is also not included in the *Souvenirs*, such as Dumas's sprain when his horse falters or several anecdotes about logistical problems, or about lack of discipline in the army. Conversely, some details appear in the *Souvenirs* that do not appear in the draft. For example, he describes that during the march to New York, he established his "bivouac" near Béville in a very pleasant location, "between rocks and under magnificent tulip trees[57]."

---

56 Dumas, *Souvenirs*, Vol. 1 p. 78. See: Rochambeau, Jean-Baptiste-Donatien de Vimeur, and J.-Charles-J Luce de Lancival. *Mémoires Militaires, Historiques et Politiques de Rochambeau: Ancien Maréchal de France, et Grand Officier* de la *Légion d'Honneur*. Fain, 1809.
57 Dumas. *Souvenirs*, vol. 1 p.70.

Translator Notes

Dumas's penmanship is very difficult to read and one can go bug-eyed very quickly. Iris de Rode did a masterful job transcribing the manuscript into print, making this translation immensely easier. As this is a draft manuscript which researchers may want to compare with other documents or to study Dumas's writing style. We thought it appropriate to translate the document as integrally as possible.

Editors generally skip over strikeouts or indicate the fact in square brackets. Readers don't know whether the strikeout involves a single word, a line, a paragraph or more. We indicate how many words or lines were deleted. If they are legible, we translate the crossed out text and put it in square brackets.

Sometimes, one can deduce the word from the initial letters and the context. When this is not possible, or if a word or sequence of words cannot be read due to faded ink or bleeding through the page, the text is marked as "illegible." Sometimes, characters are somewhat legible but their combination cannot be understood. Consonants like m, n, u, v, w, and vowels like a, e, o can often look alike in penmanship and sometimes be difficult to interpret. Such cases are indicated as "unintelligible." Text that is not clear or could have multiple meanings is indicated with a question mark if not positively clear or it is discussed in the notes.

Every language has its own idioms or expressions that don't translate well into another language, such as "raining cats and dogs." A literal translation doesn't make sense and finding suitable equivalents can sometimes be difficult. (The French equivalent is "raining buckets.") Dumas frequently uses the expression "sur le champ," literally, "on the field." Translators might use the equivalent "on the spot." The sense is one of urgency, so we use the word "immediately."

The translators of Lafayette's correspondence include a love letter to his wife Adrienne which has Lafayette and his wife building castles of happiness and pleasure in France[58]. The expression *construire châteaux en Espagne* means to daydream, so Lafayette is actually saying he spends a lot of time daydreaming about his wife.

Language changes over time and words take on different meanings. In the 17th and 18th centuries, the model or ideal for a gentleman was that of *l'honnête homme*. Today, the adjective means honest in the sense of not a cheater, but, in the 17th and 18th centuries, it had the connotation of kindness, benevolence or honorable. Medieval knights followed the ideal of *l'honnête homme* in serving their fellow humans with kindness. The characteristic persisted in the conduct of a gentleman or gentle man.

The word "*agréable*" resembles the English word "agreeable" and translators often translate it as such. However, when one uses the adjective in talking about the countryside, or even people, a more proper term to use is "pleasant," "fine" or "lovely." There are also many French words that look like English words but mean something very different. For example, "soldats blessés" does not mean blessed soldiers but wounded soldiers. One might assume that "luxure" means luxury, but it means lust. The French word for luxury is "luxe." The word "défendre" usually means to defend, but it can also mean to forbid.

Some words change meaning by changing the gender or the accent. For example, *ma mémoire* means my memory but *mon mémoire* means my memoir. Pêcheur means a fisherman while pécheur is a sinner. Also, the same word may have different meanings depending on the way it is used. For example, in the phrase *l'ennemi fort nombreux*, one might translate the word fort as an adjective: a strong and numerous enemy but here it is used as an adverb to mean "very" so the phrase should be translated as "a very numerous enemy."

---

58 Lafayette, Marie Joseph Paul Yves Roch Gilbert Du Motier. Memoirs, Correspondence and Manuscripts of General Lafayette. Saunders and Otley, 1837 vol. 1. p. 146 Lafayette, Marie Joseph Paul Yves Roch Gilbert Du Motier, and Stanley J Idzerda. Lafayette in the Age of the American Revolution : Selected Letters and Papers, 1776-1790. Cornell University Press, 1977. Vol. 1 p. 226.

Sebastien Le Prestre de Vauban (1633–1707) was the brilliant military theoretician of the 17th century. He revolutionized military engineering by designing star-shaped forts and siege warfare with zigzag trenches. His engineering principles were taught at the military academy at Mézières[59], France and remained in general use until well after the Napoleonic era in the 19th century. Consequently, much military terminology still uses French terms: abatis, bayonet (invented in Bayonne, France), chandeliers, chevaux-de-frise, demilune, fascines, flèche, fraise, gabions, glacis, parley, parole, ravelin, redan, saucissons, sortie, etc.

Sometimes words have different meanings in a military context. For example, demilune means a half-moon. In the military, it does not refer to the phase of the moon but to a fortification or a gun battery shaped like a half moon. Saucissons normally means sausages, but in a military context, it refers to long bundles of sticks tied together to strengthen fortifications because they look somewhat like sausages. Robert Burn's *A Naval and Military Technical Dictionary of the French Language: In Two Parts: French-English and English-French; with Explanations of the Various Terms*[60] was very useful in selecting proper English equivalents for many such terms.

Army regiments had two elite units the grenadiers and chasseurs who protected the wings or sides of the regiments. Dumas often speaks of these two companies together. The grenadiers were usually positioned on the left and the chasseurs on the right. The grenadiers were the shock troops. One had to be 5' 8" tall to be a member. The bearskin cap, which was abolished in 1776, added another 8 to 12 inches to their height, making them look ominous. They were usually called out to quell riots and to maintain peace. The company got its name because the men used to carry hand grenades. Grenades were no longer used in the army in the 18th

---

59 Mézières is a town in northeastern France on the Meuse River. It merged with the town on the other side of the river in 1966 and is now known as Charleville-Mézières.
60 Burn, Robert. *A Naval and Military Technical Dictionary of the French Language: In Two Parts: French-English and English-French; with Explanations of the Various Terms.* 5th ed., J. Murray, 1870.

century, but the company kept its name and the men still carried a brass matchbox on their cross belt which formerly contained the slow match to light the grenades. Grenadiers and chasseurs wore mustaches as signs of their elite status in a line regiment. Lauzun's hussars also wore mustaches.

The chasseurs were light infantrymen who acted as scouts and rangers to clear the way for the army. They patrolled the line of march to flush out snipers or to eliminate any opposition. The term chasseurs, like the German jaegers, means hunters and many translators use that term or the word chasseurs. Since they were light infantrymen, we will use the term light infantry.

The terms Tory and Negro have come to be considered derogatory and politically incorrect. We considered using Loyalist instead of Tory. However, we decided to continue to use Tory because that is the term Dumas uses and we don't think anybody would take offense with it today. We also retained the term Negro for the same reason and because some people take offense with the designation African-American, as not all people of color are of African origin.

Proper names of places and people are often misspelled or spelled phonetically, as was common in the 18th century. Sometimes, places undergo name changes. Dumas sometimes uses several variant spellings for the same names. This translation uses personal names as commonly spelled in American reference works and modern place names. Variant spellings and earlier names are specified in the notes.

Dumas consistently uses two titles to refer to individuals, such as Mr. the Count…, Mr. the Baron…, etc. The custom in the English language is to use only one title, so we will drop the Mr. and retain the title of nobility.

Norman Desmarais, Bertrand Van Ruymbeke, Iris De Rode

1781

Draft for the Campaign Diary from June 16
at the Providence camp

> May Guardian angels their kind wing display
> and be your guide in every dangerous way
> May all your future life be blessed with peace
> And every day your spring of joy increase
> in every state may your mood happy be
> and when far distant sometimes think of me
> could my hand hold the finest hand
> who wrote these above lines.

June

June 16, after finishing all the business with which I was entrusted at the Providence headquarters, I received the following instructions and pieces from Mr. de Béville[61]:

-the list of encampments
-the plan and the detail of the march

---

61 Pierre François de Béville (1721-1798) was Quartermaster General of the Army.

-detailed instructions on what I must do in going ahead to Hartford.

- the list of general officers and other attachés to the four different divisions to mark the quarters in an appropriate manner.

I wrote to my father, my uncle[62] and to Mr. de Puységur[63]. I put all my affairs in order. I left.

This book will be filled with my business and my thoughts.

I left Providence on the 17th and I went to sleep in Windham where I found Dr. Eldeshrin[64], I immediately sent a good courier[?] to Plainfield with orders to wait for Mr. de Béville. I gave him a letter for the general to whom I send the note about the quarters I marked for him at Windham. On the 18th, I marked the headquarters of the first division. I wrote a letter to Mr de Béville about his passage to Bolton.

It is said that the Loyalists allied with the savages are ravaging the region around Albany.

The Army recruits numbering 600 were incorporated into the Providence camp the night of the 16th. I came to sleep at Bolton and I reconnoitered the location of the camp in front of White's Tavern[65].

The 19 in Bolton

---

62 I initially translated this as "to my father's uncle and to Mr. de Puységur" as there is no comma in the manuscript between father and uncle. However, Dumas mentions not having the time to write to "my father and my uncle" and to Mr. de P. on August 19, so I add a comma here and conclude he wrote three letters instead of two.

63 Lieutenant General Louis Pierre de Chastenet, comte de Puységur (1727–1807) was inspector of infantry in 1776 and later became Minister of War in 1788. Dumas served as his aide-de-camp in 1777.

64 Dr. Jedediah Elderkin (1717-1793) of Windham, CT was a lawyer, States Attorney for Windham County, member of the General Assembly, one of the Governor's Council of Safety, a large land owner and a manufacturer.

65 Oliver White's Tavern 2 Brandy Street Bolton, CT. 41.77015577199059, -72.42427477611467

Here, I marked the headquarters of the first division. I wrote to Mr. de Béville about his passage to Bolton, sending him the state of the region.

In East Hartford

I arrived here at noon. I found Mr. Barnard[66], Deputy Barracks Master for Hartford and East Hartford. Together, we both reconnoitered and marked the headquarters for the first two divisions. I found even more enemies and difficulties in this operation than in any other location because the people are suspicious[67] because we took their meeting house to use as a hospital and because here, as elsewhere, there is no tolerance for the cause of a tolerant God.

In Hartford, on the 20th

I stopped and put the state of the quarters at East Hartford in order. I assured myself of the quantity of boats necessary to cross the river and I marked the pastures on this side for the artillery horses and I wrote to Mr. Béville about these different matters in a letter which will be handed to him on his passage to East Hartford.
I received good and bad news here.
General Greene[68] forced Lord Rawdon[69] to evacuate Camden[70]. The British left their wounded there and withdrew in great haste. They have successively lost all the forts northwest of Charlestown[71] and they will undoubtedly be obliged to withdraw to this place.

---

66 Ebenezer Barnard, Jr. (1752 - 1827)
67 The author uses the word "superstitieux" which is usually translated as "superstitious." However, as there is no context of religion here, the word "suspicious" seems more appropriate as the context is one of mistrust.
68 Major General Nathanael Greene (1742–1786) commanded the Continental Army in the South.
69 Lord Francis Rawdon-Hastings, 1st Marquess of Hastings (1754–1826) commanded the British left wing at the Battle of Camden. When Cornwallis went into Virginia, he left Rawdon in effective command in the South.
70 Battle of Camden August 16, 1780.
71 Charleston, SC

Augusta and Ninety-Six[72] are invested but Cornwallis[73], who withdrew on his right as far as Wilmington, had left Lord Rawdon to block, stop and occupy. General Greene marched with such haste that he is actually 40 miles from Williamsburg[74] with 6000 effective men, having rejoined the body of troops commanded by Arnold[75]. The Marquis de Lafayette[76] is 100 miles to the northwest of him awaiting the reinforcements General Wayne[77] is bringing him.

I marked the quarters of the general officers at Hartford[78] and I reserved enough space for the people, whom the general will allow to depart, to return from East Hartford.

In East Hartford, on the 21st

Mr. Béville arrived here this morning preceded by the detachment of workers. We passed the day reconnoitering different locations for the camp. The general set that of the first two divisions below and facing the village about ½ mile [away].

We learn at this time and we will announce to the Comte de Rochambeau[79] that Arnold has returned to New York with 200 horses and a few light recruits, that Admiral Arbuthnot is ready to

---

72 Ninety-Six, SC. 34.173211, -82.021710 Major General Nathanael Greene besieged this fort with 1,000 Continental Army troops from May 22 to June 18, 1781.
73 General Charles Cornwallis (1738–1805) British general who surrendered at Yorktown Oct. 19, 1781.
74 Williamsburg was the capital of the Virginia Colony from 1699 to 1780. 37.27597459962942, -76.7025213274497
75 Benedict Arnold (1741–1801) had betrayed the post of West Point by this time and was leading a band of Crown forces on a march of destruction in the South.
76 Major General Marie Jean Paul Joseph du Motier Marquis de Lafayette (1757–1834) was a French volunteer in the Continental Army. Dumas routinely spells his name de la Fayette.
77 Brigadier General Anthony" Wayne (1745–1796) received the nickname "Mad Anthony" because of his order to attack the fort at Stony Point, NY with unloaded muskets and fixed bayonets.
78 The Hartford camp was on the east bank of the Connecticut River. 41.774360780525306, -72.65032743193716
79 Jean Baptiste Donatien de Vimeur, comte de Rochambeau (1725-1807) was the French general who commanded the expedition particulière.

set sail with a convoy of a large number of empty transport ships, that the enemy has reinforced the post of Kingsbridge and that he is preparing to send a large detachment to the continent. We suppose that the purpose of these movements is to forage which is absolutely necessary for them and which our arrival would at least make it doubtful.

At East Hartford on the 22

The first division of the army arrived early this morning, having encountered so far very little delay. The general marched at the rear of the column. After reconnoitering the camp, the Comte de Rochambeau went to Hartford where he took his quarters at Colonel Wadsworth's[80].

I went to reconnoiter a plot to camp and to park the artillery on the other side of the city of Hartford, at the fork of the Wethersfield and Farmington roads. The army was to march by the latter.

The artillery division and the baggage of the general officers crossed the river in very little time.

If military discipline is an equal and successive chain, it is necessary that the first scout be the strongest. Let us agree on XXX and the protests, the discussion of rights, the search for rest and indecent plans are directly opposed to every military principle – this to make me remember a little scene.

In Hartford on the 23rd

The 2nd division arrived this morning. Monsieur le Comte de Vioménil[81] went to Hartford. Everything else was the same as with

---

80 Jeremiah Wadsworth (1743–1804) was an American sea captain, merchant, and statesman from Hartford, Connecticut who profited from his position as a government official charged with supplying the French Army.
81 Antoine Charles du Houx baron de Vioménil (1728-1792) was second-in-command of the expeditionary force sent to America.

the first division. I handed over to the Chevalier de Lameth[82] the quarters of the second and third divisions. And I reconnoitered and marked the camp for the third.

The general first planned to go meet General Washington[83] in person, but the latest news about the enemy and the detachment he planned to send out from Kingsbridge made him decide not to leave the army. We think the general will come before the army at Newtown[84].

The route of the left column was changed a bit. The roads through Oxford were deemed impracticable, so the Legion leaves Lebanon[85] today and will rejoin at Middletown[86] with a Mr. who performs the functions of assistant quartermaster general for this column.

Major Tallmage[87], an American dragoon officer, noted for his talents and his invasion of Long Island at the end of the last campaign and whose face bears the character of the reputation he merited, had a conversation with the Comte de Rochambeau and I served as his interpreter for a time. He assured the general that Sheldon's Dragoon Regiment had mustered at Bedford and that

---

82 Alexandre-Théodore-Victor, comte de Lameth (1760-1829) served as one of Rochambeau's aides-de-camp and assistant quartermaster general. He was elected to the Estates General and advocated for the abolition of clergy privileges. He became colonel of the fifth regiment of horse guards in 1791 and major general in 1792. He was imprisoned until 1797. He returned to France in 1799, became prefect in 1804, and Peer of France in 1820.
83 General George Washington (1732-1799) was commander in chief of the Continental Army.
84 Newtown, CT is east of Danbury. The camp was at the Caleb Baldwin Tavern, 32 Main Street 41.4130031792673, -73.3081624896231
85 Lauzun's Legion had its winter quarters on the Lebanon Green 149 W Town St, Lebanon, CT, 41.63690791774765, -72.2198716165212, near Captain Joseph Trumble's Store and Office known as the Revolutionary War Office.
86 Middletown, CT 41.56791610662671, -72.7252367177065 is about 14 miles south of Hartford.
87 Benjamin Tallmadge (1754-1835) was a major in the 2nd Continental Light Dragoons and the head of General Washington's spy ring known as the Culper Ring.

there were several detachments ordered to precede and cover the march of the French army.

I received a verbal instruction from Mr. de Béville to precede him and to continue to make the initial reconnaissance.

My brother[88] was sent to Peekskill to get news of the layout of the forces. He must have been quick and he will return to the army. We are happy about his activity. We encourage him only with encouragement because that is the only way for people of honor.

At Southington on the 24th

I left Hartford this morning with Mr. de Béville. I reconnoitered the camp and the quarters at Farmington[89] with him. I left him there and pushed as far as this camp which is the second march from Hartford. I reconnoitered the camp and the closest houses. I left a list for Mr. de Béville and I'm leaving for Breakneck[90].

This evening I took an hour during which I must remember the positions, ["the course" crossed out] the vessels and what I went to see with great pleasure and some regrets.

At Newtown on the 25th

I went to Breakneck where Captain Bronson showed me the land where the wood and the straw were gathered. It appeared to me to be too narrow and in a poor location. I had a list of houses drawn up which will be given to Mr. de Béville on his arrival.

I encountered my brother along the way who made extreme haste and who was running to warn Mr. -- the comptroller[91] that

---

88 Guillaume Mathieu Dumas de St Marcel, (1755-1826) served as a served as a lieutenant in the régiment provincial de Montpellier.
89 The camp at Farmington was at Major Peter Curtis Tavern, 4 High Street. 41.72469297924009, -72.8230194896101
90 Breakneck is now Middlebury. The camp was at the home of Josiah Bronson at 506 Breakneck Hill Road. 41.547558549736515, -73.12432028961751
91 Benoit Joseph de Tarlé (1735-1797) was comptroller general of the expedition particulière.

nothing is ready at Peekskill. The ovens are not yet built and we must surely delay the army's arrival two or three days at that point.

I have nothing to say about the region I cross rapidly. The plan of march and the excellent itinerary Mr. de Béville gave me are full of topographical details. From Barnes' Tavern[92] to here, the country is hilly, varied and full of these irregularities which I like. I noticed a wooden bridge[93] over the Stratford 4 miles from here constructed on a new model. All the weight bearing on the upper structure is sent to the abutments because of the angle of the buttresses and their double strength due to the pieces which support the beams.

The location of Newtown is very pleasant. This village is full of Tories. I was given the names of several well-intentioned people and warned to be on my guard.

I learned here that the largest part of General Washington's army was camped at Peekskill and that it had already [crossed out word] sent a detachment of about 600 men to White Plains under the command of Colonel Scammell[94].

At Newtown on the 26th

Colonel Chandler[95], to whom I was addressed and where I took my quarters, accompanied me this morning on the reconnaissance of a terrain suitable to camp the four divisions and the necessary quarters for the entire general staff of the army. The order of march was changed at Hartford. It was decided that the four divisions

---

92 Barnes Tavern, 1089 Marion Ave, Plantsville, CT 41.5681152601551,-72.9243660761231 was the camp prior to the Breakneck one.
93 Carleton's Bridge. Louis François Bertrand Dupont d'Aubevoye, comte de Lauberdière, Journal de l'Armée aux ordres de Monsieur de Comte de Rochambeau pendant les campagnes de 1780, 1781, 1782, 1783 dans l'Amérique septentrionale has an illustration of the bridge.
http://gallica.bnf.fr/ark:/12148/btv1b52506900t/f17.image. Fol. 89
94 Colonel Alexander Scammell (1747–1781) Adjutant-General of the American armies and Colonel of the First New Hampshire Regiment.
95 Colonel John Chandler (1736-1796) served as the lieutenant colonel of Gold Selleck Silliman's regiment of Connecticut militia levies.

would join here and that we would then march by regiment all the way to the camp at Peekskill.

It appeared to me that the most suitable place for the camp was mid-hill in the area east of the meetinghouse, in the open pastures of little value, with the Stratford Road on its right and the brook to furnish water for the camp on the left. We could camp the four divisions in a single line.

In this position, we face the enemy. We can cover the right flank and the headquarters, which is located a little behind the right, by bringing a corps of grenadiers and light infantry[96] on the height that commands the city and from which we can view the whole region. The post of the advance guard in this position would be on a hill 1 mile south of the church which dominates the exterior valley beyond the hill where the grenadiers and light infantrymen would be camped.

We could also take the camp by facing the city and in this case, we would camp in two lines, approaching the brook as much as possible with the artillery in front. But, in this case, the headquarters would be ahead of the camp and would necessarily need to be covered by the above-mentioned hill.

I reconnoitered a communication post of the grenadiers and light infantry on the Danbury Road, along which the army must pass.

The 27th at Newtown

Mr. de Béville arrived this morning. He reconnoitered the region and had the camp marked on two lines in the rear on both sides of

---

96 Each regiment was composed of 10 companies of 70 to 100 men. Eight of those companies were soldats (infantrymen). The other two were the elite companies of grenadiers and chasseurs (light infantry) which were usually placed on each end of the line, the grenadiers on the left and the chasseurs on the right. The grenadiers were the shock troops called out for police action, to break up riots, quell insurrections, etc. Often, just the appearance of the grenadiers was enough to dispel a crowd. One had to be at least 5 feet 8 inches tall to be in this company and the bearskin cap which was abolished in 1776 added another 8+ inches. The chasseurs acted as scouts and were used to flush out snipers and to clear the line of march.

the brook, the grenadiers and light infantry on the hill above the city.

The 28th at Newtown

The Comte de Rochambeau arrived with the first division. I accompanied him on the various reconnaissances.

The 29th at Newtown

The second division arrived. I received the order to go mark the housing at Ridgebury[97] and Crompond and to reconnoiter a camp for the army. Mr. de Béville gave me an order. I wrote to...

The 30th at Hunt's Tavern[98]

I posted to Ridgebury and I reconnoitered the site of a camp for the first regiment below the church and a camp for the grenadiers and light infantry beyond, on a height which dominates the Salem Valley. I wrote to Mr. de Béville, sending him a list of houses for the general and his family before sleeping at Hunt's Tavern.

This place is 12 miles above Bedford and 8 miles from Crompond[99] and at the entrance to the gorges which lead to White Plains. This whole region is desolated by the refugee Tories called cowboys because they are primarily employed by the British to steal cattle and to bring them to New York. The American dragoons had

---

97 The Ridgebury camp was at Ensign Samuel Keeler's Tavern, 152 Main Street, Ridgefield, CT 41.273222639299526, -73.49678950513994

98 Hunt's Tavern was the site of the Crompond camp. The tavern stood on the north side of Crompond Road near the intersection with Hallock's Mill Road, east of the Crompond and Mohansic Lakes. The camp was along the north side of Baldwin Road between SR 202 and Hallocks Mill Road. 41.27950265030544, -73.78821065518697. Dumas writes it as Heitz Tavern. Other sources write it as Height's Tavern. Salem Valley doesn't appear by that name in any of the period or modern maps but it is probably where Hallock's Mill Brook runs 41.28665309446964, -73.78358173572039. The grenadier and light infantry camp was probably on the west side of Sultana Drive.

99 Crompond is now Yorktown Heights, NY. 41.27950265030544, -73.78821065518697.

restrained them a little during the last campaigns, but we have not yet been able to prevent the constant communication between the continent and New York. It is not surprising that this fine part of the state of New York is full of people sold to the British government. They were the first and the most entirely deprived of every commerce by the North River[100]. They constantly supported the weight of the war and lacked everything. Under the strongest hand, they gave up and followed the only party that could sustain them. It seems to me that the presence of the French army has already had some effect on gaining the confidence of the good Americans and the Tories almost refuse to live here any more.

General Washington's army is camped at Peekskill[101]. The Comte de Rochambeau has already received several expresses from him. This is the first time our operations will be jointly concerted.

The small region I find myself in is almost entirely inhabited by Dutch families. This is in the Highlands. The mountains are not as high as near Fishkill Landing. The lands are well cultivated. There is much wheat. The vistas are very pleasant. We only regret that such good land is so cruelly ravaged.

---

100 The North River is another name for the Hudson River and both are used interchangeably.
101 The Peekskill camp, called Continental Village, was along the south side of Crompond Road between Washington Street and Lafayette Avenue. 41.27323849784073, -73.91577911708491

Fig. 1. Grenadier of the Bourbonnais Regiment (note mustache). Soldats (infantry soldiers) would be uniformed similarly but were required to be clean shaven. Troops in the Saintonge and Soissonnais regiments would have similar uniforms. Instead of black colored facings (lapels and cuffs), the Soissonnais would have salmon and the Saintonge green.

Dress Regulations 21 February 1779 (*Règlement Arrêté par le Roi, pour l'Habillement et l'Équipement de ses Troupes du 21 Février 1779*. Paris: l'Imprimerie Royale, 1779). Engraving by Nicholas Hoffman.

Fig. 2. Régiment Saintonge. L to R. soldat, ensign (flag bearer), drummer, grenadier (note the mustache and grenade on the bottom of his coat). Chasseurs (light infantryman) would have a bugle emblem instead of the grenade. Soldats (infantry soldiers) would be uniformed similarly, except that the bottoms of their regimental coats would have a fleur-de-lis. The two figures in the rear, in salmon-colored facings, are in the Régiment Soissonnais.

July

July 1 at Ridgebury

I left Hunt's Tavern this morning with the general of the state of New York[102]. I first reconnoitered the planned location for the army camp. I found its position to be poor and inconvenient militarily speaking. From there, I went to Crompond where the lack of water led me to the same conclusion about this place, but I reconnoitered one on the left of the road 2 miles away and on the crest of Pines Bridge[103] which would be both strong and convenient. I then returned to Armonk[104] where I reported to Mr. de Béville in a letter that I wrote according to his instruction.

I had barely sealed the letter when I received a messenger from the general who ordered me to depart for Cottonville[105] to go find him at Ridgebury. I had already suspected a change in tomorrow's march, in effect that of the American army which should be prepared to move tomorrow at 2 or 3 o'clock in the morning.

I immediately departed for Ridgebury. I encountered Sheldon's dragoons who had orders to go to Bedford and beyond to push the bands of Tories who might remain in the valleys toward New York.

---

102 Pierre Van Cortlandt served as the first Lieutenant Governor of New York and was re-elected several times between 1777–1795
103 Now Yorktown Heights, NY. 41.22744009432569, -73.77692817405577
104 Armonk was more commonly called Mile Square in the 18th century. 41.127032842355206, -73.71490476079946
105 Unidentified location.

I arrived here at night when I received the general's order for the first brigade to march toward Bedford.

I bivouacked and...

2 at Upper Salem[106]

I left [Bedford crossed out] Ridgebury at 2 o'clock in the morning with Mr. de Béville. Upon arriving at Bedford[107], we reconnoitered the site of the camp on a spacious and open plateau. On this side of the gorge, the grenadiers and light infantry [camped] on a hill in the middle of the valley, commanding the entire region and cutting the road to New York, that to Norwalk and that of North Castle[108]. The general arrived and approved this arrangement and soon after Lauzun's Legion arrived at Ridgefield, the last point by which the left column would have to travel before joining the army.

Lauzun's Legion is in the best state. The Duc de Lauzun[109], commanding this advanced corps joined with that of Colonel Sheldon[110] will precede with special instructions.

I received an order from Mr. de Béville to go immediately with the Chevalier de Lameth to reconnoiter the communication of Bedford with North Castle, to assign a proper camp for a brigade and even for the army to observe the position well and to then go to as far as [3 words crossed out] Ridgebury by a different route than the one we came this morning [in order to] take the second brigade

---

106 North Salem
107 Present-day Bedford Village 41.197564826709055, -73.6169771700678
108 Mount Kisco today.
109 Armand Louis de Gontaut-Biron, Duc de Lauzun (1747–1793) commanded a legion of cavalry and infantry composed of foreign volunteers (a French Foreign Legion). They were attached to the navy and played a decisive role in the siege of Yorktown. Consequently, Lauzun was charged with bringing the news of the victory back to France to King Louis XVI.
110 Colonel Elisha Sheldon (1740–1805) raised and commanded the 2nd Continental Light Dragoons, known as "Sheldon's Horse." He served with distinction throughout the Revolutionary War. The town of Sheldon, Vermont was named for him.

and lead it by this road to North Castle if I deemed this new route better.

I left immediately. We even excavated, reconnoitered the site to the best of our ability and reported in writing that 4 battalions could camp comfortably in two lines, each on the plateau to the right of the church with a rather large brook, in front of the camp, which has its source in a marsh in front of the church and behind the left of the position.

The grenadiers and light infantry could camp on the hill above the marsh which plunges into the Tarrytown and White Plains roads, 12 miles from Tarrytown and 15 miles to White Plains.

I inquired which was the most direct route from North Castle to Ridgebury. I was told it was the one from[111] and Upper Salem. I took a guide as far as the first of these places and then I took 2 different ones to assure myself as much as possible from one or the other in a region where everyone is suspect.

I made great haste and arrived at Upper Salem at nightfall. I expected to get a relay there as my horse faltered and I fell underneath, still in the saddle. My foot was so badly trampled before I was able to disengage myself that it was impossible to mount a horse. I arrived at the first house with difficulty. From here, I sent an express to the Comte de Vioménil, sending him Mr. de Béville's order and requesting the encampments to which I would assign a guide.

3 at North Castle

Mr. Collot[112] arrived at the house where I was staying at 2 o'clock in the morning, cursing my bad luck. I gave him a guide and he departed to stake out the route.

---

111   The troops followed the Old Post Road but the words don't look anything like that. Louis Alexandre Berthier's map does not show this part of the route. The first brigade marched from Ridgebury to North Castle by way of Bedford. The second brigade went by Bedford Center.

112   Georges Henri Victor Collot (1750-1805) served as one of the Count de Rochambeau's aides and then as quartermaster for Lauzun's Legion.

An hour later, the Comte de Vioménil arrived with the 2nd brigade. The surgeon loaned me his cabriolet after examining me and I marched thus, conducting the column all the way to North Castle, a long and difficult march for the soldiers in excessive heat.

The entire army is reunited at North Castle. The march from Providence to here was conducted orderly, speedily and with courage. We left very few men behind. The Saintonge Regiment lost none, neither from exhaustion nor from desertion, despite the difficulties of the terrain. The artillery and the baggage both arrived in good time. All the camps were supplied abundantly. Finally, the service was done, the temporary order at hand with the latest updates, and this joyous execution was the proof. This is probably the first French troop overseas that maintained this discipline and regularity against which so many people have rebelled during the last peace and to which we must certainly owe [crossed out and overwritten] our successes. The Comte de Rochambeau can flatter himself for this perfect harmony which he maintained in his army, a unity on which the various opinions and special interests, united or divided, can have no bearing.

4 at North Castle

We asked ourselves for two days where was the American army? Where did the Duc de Lauzun go? Why did we gain a march? The Comte de Rochambeau received some dispatches from the Comte de Fersen[113] and the Marquis of Vauban[114], his aides de camp whom he permitted to accompany the Duc de Lauzun to his first detachment. We knew that the enemy only had a body of about 300 light troops beyond Kingsbridge, that the garrison of Fort Washington[115]

---

113 Hans Axel von, comte de Fersen (1755-1810), Swedish aide-de-camp in Rochambeau's army and assistant quartermaster general.
114 Jacques Anne Joseph le Prestre, comte de Vauban (1754-1815) was one of Rochambeau's aides-de-camp.
115 Fort Washington was on the eastern side of the Hudson River, south of where the George Washington Bridge is and opposite Fort Lee, NJ. When the Crown forces captured it, they renamed it Fort Knyphausen. 40.8487479051861, -73.944355876338

was very weak and that the greatest part of the regular troops was on Long Island. General Washington wanted to attempt to surprise the fort and since the British, informed of our successive marches, believed we had arrived at Peekskill to join the American army. These, embarked on the North River, gained a march and landed a few miles above Kingsbridge. General Lincoln[116] was to land on the very island of New York and to attempt to capture the fort, sword in hand. The Duc de Lauzun with his Legion, 170 of Sheldon's men, and the 600 men under the command of General Waterbury[117] were to fall upon the body of light troops whose retreat on the island was blocked.

The enemies were advised of our movements. General Lincoln was forced to land above Kingsbridge[118] because he was discovered and he learned that the garrison of the fort had been reinforced. He then concentrated on attacking the advance posts at Kingsbridge. He was to attack the left at the same time that Lauzun's Legion would attack the right. In effect, the Legion marched all night and arrived at William's Bridge[119] that very day. They crossed it and went to reconnoiter the enemy position. They were more numerous than supposed and as soon as they spotted the Legion on the hills across the Bronx, they put themselves in motion.

The infantry, in column, attempted to turn the Duc de Lauzun's right and about 170 dragoons advanced on his front. The Duke

---

116 Major General Benjamin Lincoln (1733–1810) was involved in three major surrenders during the war: his participation in the Battles of Saratoga contributed to John Burgoyne's surrender of a British army. He oversaw the largest American surrender of the war at the 1780 Siege of Charleston, and, as George Washington's second in command, he formally accepted the British surrender at Yorktown.
117 General David Waterbury (1722–1801) commanded part of the Connecticut First Division. He joined with the main body of the Continental Army under General Washington in the summer of 1781.
118 Kingsbridge, also spelled King's Bridge and Kings Bridge, was the northernmost outpost of the Crown forces on York (Manhattan) Island. 40.88172479090685, -73.90565120104297 It was strategically important in the New York campaign and the start of the Yorktown campaign.
119 Williamsbridge is a neighborhood in the north-central portion of the Bronx in New York City 40.877000, -73.866000.

recrossed the Bronx and then General Lincoln began his attack with an inferior force. The engagement was quite heated. The Americans had 20 men killed and about 300 wounded at the head of the columns. General Washington had the time to make a very detailed reconnaissance of the works at Kingsbridge during the battle and approached to within musket range.

The forts fired cannon at him. General Lincoln withdrew to the American army which supported him. General Washington, after having made the reconnaissance which was his principal object, had his army and Lauzun's Legion march to take a position at White Plains, about 12 miles from Kingsbridge.

5 at North Castle

The order was given last night to march to camp at White Plains, on the left of the American army, but a counter-order was given during the night, and this morning General Washington arrived here where he visited the position and the posts of the French army. We learned nothing, or at least said nothing, about the enemies. The Americans are very pleased with us, but they are not very enthusiastic about the strength of our support. There is not a single countryman who doesn't ask how many vessels will arrive to attack New York.

The 6th at the White Plains camp near Philipsburg

The army departed North Castle this morning to come camp here, a march of 18 miles in unbearable heat. The grenadiers and light infantry and the encampments were at the head, the artillery of these regiments, the baggage and artillery following the same order and in a single column. As I am barely able to mount a horse, I haven't been charged with anything. I followed the encampments by little steps and, upon arriving, I met the allied generals who wandered along the front of the land reserved for the French camp. I was very pleased to find myself near the Comte de Rochambeau at the moment General Washington arrived on the highest butte, showing him the general position and the different ways he could capture it which he left to his choice. General Rochambeau decided on the first camp which was more military, but less well-aligned with the American camp. Here is an overview such as I heard it from the very mouth of General Washington whom I served as interpreter. When I am able to run, I will make a detailed inspection.

The hills of Philipsburg which we occupied are 4 miles from White Plains They dominate the entire region as far as New York and cut the span between the Bronx and the North River, which is about 6 miles, about 12 miles north of Kingsbridge. The left of the position occupied by the French army abuts the Bronx and is separated from it by slopes which diminish all the way to the bed of this river. Between them and the left is a road that leads to New York. There is also a road which follows the course of the North River which is on the right of the American army.

The 7th same

There was a little confusion yesterday when the troops arrived because, marching in a single column, they arrived almost at the same time as the camps. The generals had not yet determined the ground. Mr. de Béville also could neither survey the camp nor open the principal communications. The changes of orders and plans about the meeting point necessarily resulted in some delay in provisions. The quarters were not marked before the arrival of the troops as they were always done previously. And if we complained much, we yelled at everybody a lot. One must be greatly accustomed to people and have much experience in this job to not be moved by the unjust and unreasonable complaints. It is often very difficult to do one's duty despite the unrest and obsessive ignorants.

It was decided that from the day after tomorrow [crossed out and overwritten], we would go forage by regiment. Mr. de Béville had a reconnaissance done on this matter.

Communications were open in every direction and a principal one between the American and the French lines.

I am still lame, useless, unable to see the American army, the officers I know there and thousands of things that interest me.

Nothing is said of Virginia, nothing about the South and nothing about Ste. Lucie.

Mr.[120] arrived here last night.

The 8th same

General Washington reviewed both armies today. When we were on the right of the first American line, he stood there and saluted General Rochambeau who did the same thing at the right of the French line.

We estimate the American troops at 4000 effective men under arms, not counting the detached posts and the forward guards. They are mostly poorly clad, but good under arms. Military bearing and all the officers have the best possible appearance. This junction of the French and American troops is an interesting time. Up to now, we cannot ask for a more perfect agreement among them.

9 same

This morning we reconnoitered a forage for the army about 2 miles in front of our first posts. It was a failure because we were not provided with scythes and the order which must be maintained in these types of operation was not observed this first time.

We received news of the Marquis de Lafayette: Cornwallis withdrew more than 100 miles toward the coast. His rearguard was attacked and pursued with advantage by the Marqus de Lafayette's advance guard commanded by General Wayne[121].

---

120   Anne-César de la Luzerne (1741-1791) succeeded Conrad Alexandre Gérard de Rayneval as the French Minister to the United States and later served as the official Ambassador of France until 1784.
121   The Battle of Green Spring (VA) July 6, 1781.

10 same

Our camp is well seated. It does not appear that we need to constantly take a position closer to the enemy. The movement of the army, the proximity of the enemy and the certainty of acting have not quelled the discontent nor melded the spirits. Many people have the honor [phrase crossed out] to find themselves here who could not complain about their duty. They disagree with those who make them do it and there are faults on all sides and reciprocal wrongs, jealousy, ambition, poor judgment, and nothing is overlooked.

The officers of the American army are already more refined in their appearance than they were before. We strive to lessen our luxury and augment theirs, which is an evil because the soldier class will suffer.

The 11th same

I reconnoitered part of the position we occupy, especially the left and the course of the Bronx[122]. The slope on our side is so steep and covered with wood that the left of the position could be completely assured. The space between this slope and the hill on which we camp is extremely secure and the post which is on the road to New York would suffice to defend the gorge.

Mr. Hamilton[123] arrived from Albany. He is no longer part of the general's family. It is said he must command a corps of light troops. Some people doubt that he is also still in the general's confidence as he seemed to be up to this time. It would be unfortunate that from such great means, so astonishing at his age, he should be useless or misdirected. His politics on the first offers of peace were considered extraordinary and light. He said the British would retain

---

122 The Bronx River, the only fresh water river in New York City, flows approximately 24 miles through southeast New York. It is named after colonial settler Jonas Bronck.
123 Alexander Hamilton (1755-1804) served four years as Washington's chief staff aide. Washington reprimanded him for a minor misunderstanding on February 15, 1781 and Hamilton left his staff.

a few of their possessions and the total independence of the United States would not be recognized by the treaty. Whatever degree of possibility that this statement might have had, we should not expect it from an American.

The 12th same

We heard a lively cannonade in the Sound[124], on the left of our camp from 3 o'clock in the morning until 10. We learned from the American patrols [phrase crossed out] that French frigates cannonaded the coast. The Comte de Rochambeau, who transmitted to Mr. de Barras[125] some intelligence about the fort[126] closing Huntington Bay on Long Island did not doubt that he undertook anything on this point.

A few British deserters came to us. Their worthless reports on the effective force of the New York garrison cannot be counted for anything.

We made another general forage today. Against all the rules of war and the economy, we would like that there be some direction of the forages during the campaign, that the forage be cut, stored and distributed according to the stipulations of this rule and by people outside the troop. However, this difference is so enormous that the Comte de Rochambeau would undoubtedly seriously restrain his hand in the execution of the order. Our reapers are few, clumsy, etc. but we must try to overcome these difficulties.

---

124   Long Island Sound. 41.09777822053028, -72.95274774285465
125   Jacques-Melchior Saint-Laurent, Comte de Barras (1719–1793) was a French naval officer promoted to head of the naval fleet. He commanded the *Zelé* in admiral d'Estaing fleet at the battle of Sainte Lucie (December 1778) and the Battle of Grenada (July 1779). He was appointed to succeed Admiral de Ternay at Newport, Rhode Island in March 1781. He left Rhode Island on August 24, 1781, his ships loaded with the siege artillery and supplies for the siege of Yorktown.
126   Fort Franklin on Lloyd Neck, NY 40.90691978861717, -73.47654645767096 or Fort Slongo at Fort Salonga, NY 40.91257430297852, -73.30039133197276.

Fig. 3. Reproduction of the French frigate *Hermione*. Translator's photo.

13 same

We learned today of the new position of the capture of Augusta by General Greene and it is also spreading that the Comte de Grasse[127] and Mr. de Bouillé[128] after having raised the siege of Ste.

---

127 Admiral François Joseph Paul Comte de Grasse (1722–1788) played a decisive role in the Yorktown campaign. After this action, he returned to the Caribbean with his fleet. British Admiral Rodney decisively defeated and captured him at the Battle of the Saintes in 1782. De Grasse was widely criticized for this loss and he demanded a court martial upon his return to France in 1784. Its verdict acquitted him of fault in the defeat.
128 François Claude Amour, marquis de Bouillé (1739-1800) was governor of the Caribbean islands of Guadeloupe, Martinique and St. Lucia. He was involved in organizing, provisioning, and leading troops in a number of actions in the West Indies. He returned to France where he held military commands in the country's northeast at the time of the French Revolution. A committed Royalist, he was a leading conspirator involved in the royal family's failed flight in 1791. This failure forced him into exile. He died in exile in London and is mentioned as a hated Royalist in the French national anthem, *La Marseillaise*.

Lucie, went to Barbados where Admiral Rodney[129] withdrew with 17 ships of the line.

It is said that the expedition of our frigates on Huntington Bay was not successful. The guard ship which covered a convoy of smaller ships had them return to the bay and set sail for New York, firing retreat cannons. The pilots did not want to undertake entering the frigates and it was not considered prudent to land the troops at night. 200 men were put ashore at dawn[130]. They went to reconnoiter the fort and found it so strong that they immediately boarded. That's all.

14 the same

The Bourbonnais Regiment, [one word crossed out] the grenadiers and light infantry of the left brigade, 1500 men of the American army, Lauzun's Legion, Sheldon's dragoons and all the campaign artillery received the order to be ready to march in four columns ahead of the front of the line. The retreat served as the general[131] but, at the time the march began, the general issued a counter-order. It was solely attributed to the bad weather which was not considered favorable for a reconnaissance which we supposed was the main object of this motion.

15 the same

We often spoke of resuming the missed part but the weather is still very poor, very foggy. Two deserters from New York arrived

---

129 Sir George Brydges Rodney (1718–1792) was a British naval officer best known for his victory over the French at the Battle of the Saintes in 1782. It is often claimed that he was the commander to have pioneered the tactic of breaking the line.
The expression "pointe du jour" is usually translated as "dawn," the first moments the sun comes up. However, since the soldiers were often on the march at 2 or 3 am, one could interpret the expression as the beginning of the day, after midnight, or "pre-dawn."
130 The expression "pointe du jour" is usually translated as "dawn," the first moments the sun comes up. However, since the soldiers were often on the march at 2 or 3 am, one could interpret the expression as the beginning of the day, after midnight, or "pre-dawn."
131 The general is a music call for camp duties.

with their weapons. They assured us that all the guards who were on the other side of the bridge had been withdrawn and only a corporal and 6 men were left there during the night.

At 9 o'clock at night, we heard cannon fire on the American right. At least that's what we thought. ["we fired" crossed out] Our alarm pieces replied. The general was beaten and the entire line took up arms. A moment later, we learned that it was some British frigates going up the North River cannonading the forts as a reprisal for our undertaking. Everybody returned and we know no more.

The 16 same

We learned this morning that two British frigates, 2 galleys and an armed boat went up the North River during the night opposite Tarrytown[132] which they cannonaded. They captured a boat which carried bread for the French army. They then tried to land some people ashore, but a detachment of Sheldon's dragoons and a French guard commanded by a sergeant made such a lively fire that the enemy were obliged to withdraw after setting fire to a small ship which they could not take with them. Captain Hurlbut[133] was wounded in the thigh.

We sent two 12 pounders and 2 howitzers[134] to the Tarrytown battery. The generals themselves went there. The frigates distanced

---

132 Tarrytown is on the east bank of the Hudson River just north of where I-87 S (I-287 E|New York State Thruway) crosses the river. A bronze tablet pas placed on the west front of the Hudson River Railroad Station. It was dedicated on July 15, 2008 to commemorate "the action of Tarrytown, which occurred near this spot on July 15, 1781, and also the heroism of Colonel Sheldon and Captain George Hurlbut of the Second Regiment of Dragoons." 41.06779524856813, -73.86494755896952

133 Captain George Hurlbut (1755 - 1783) enlisted as part of George Washington's "Life Guards." During a battle on the Hudson River (Summer, 1781), one of the American boats caught fire from a British cannon. Captain Hurlbut volunteered to swim to the boat and extinguish the fire, which he did under severe fire from the British. In returning however, he was hit in the groin by gunshot.

134 A howitzer is a cannon with a short barrel and a bore diameter greater than 30 mm and a maximum elevation of 60 degrees, used for firing shells at a high angle of elevation to reach a target behind cover or in a trench. See fig. 12.

themselves from the battery fire and remained anchored out of range in the widest part of the Tappan Sea all day.

The 17th same

The army will be lacking bread for 24 hours. Rations are reduced. It's my fault for having separated the camps so much from the provisions. The frigates went up river a few miles above Tarrytown. Two 18-pounders which we have brought up fired on the frigates. We brought 2 howitzers to the Dobbs Ferry battery, which is the narrowest point in the river, and we should also bring the 2 18-pounders which were at Tarrytown. I was at Dobbs Ferry[135] with Mr. de Béville and after seeing the new fort which we just built and the battery, we then went on a hill in front of all the American posts from whence we could see Fort Washington perfectly and part of New York island.

The 18th same

The Comte de Rochambeau and Mr. de Béville went to reconnoiter the other side of the North River. We only learned of their plan upon their return. They brought nobody with them. I was at Pines Bridge to mark and repair the communication by which the bread convoys should arrive from now on.

The frigates remained anchored at the same point. It is said that [illegible][136] landed a few [one word illegible][137] on the right bank during the generals' reconnaissance, but we sent some troops across and they recalled theirs.

The 19th same

---

135 Dobbs Ferry is about 15 miles below Kings Ferry and less than 10 miles north of Kingsbridge. It was an important crossing site on the Hudson River. As it was too close to the British defenses of New York City, the Americans used Kings Ferry which was covered by Stony Point and the works at Verplancks Point. 41.013243241575815, -73.87949261838777
136 Appears to by leppuny lasi.
137 Appears to be lrorkines.

This morning about 10 o'clock, the winds being from the northwest, pleasant and fresh, the frigates made ready and descended the river. They skirted Dobbs Ferry and the battery fire on their crossing. We lodged many bullets on board and 2 howitzer shells, one of which set fire to a frigate. The entire crew abandoned the battery to extinguish the fire. The little flotilla crowded their sails and we observed them up to their arrival at the edge of York Island.

Last night, one of the advanced posts of Lauzun's Legion was fired upon. The Duke sent out a patrol commanded by Mr. Hartmann[138]. This officer, as brave as imprudent, personally advanced on a road he did not know. Several gunshots were fired at him at close range. He fell dead. His horse returned to his troop which fired upon him. [one word crossed out]. The brigadier who was at closest range ran to him and saw a troop of armed people which he estimated at about 30 men. Behold the first small action. It would have cost an important officer.

Whether the lack of provisions delayed the detachment we were to make, or whether the plan was changed, nothing is spoken of it for several days.

The 20 same

We received a few confirmations of Mr. de Grasse's victory over Admiral Rodney. If it is as total as is said, if he captured 2 ships, we should hope to see him arrive here and to lay siege to New York.

The 21 Kingsbridge

According to the generals' order, a large detachment of both armies marched on Kingsbridge at 9 o'clock at night in the following order: 2 brigades of the American army preceded by Sheldon's dragoons and Colonel Scammell's light infantry by the Dobbs Ferry Road along the river bank; the Bourbonnais Regiment and the artillery along the road at the right of the French camp; 400 grenadiers

---

138 Jacques Hartmann (ca. 1745-1781) sous-lieutenant in Lauzun's Legion.

and light infantrymen, Lauzun's Legion and 4 pieces of cannon by the Road to Turkey Hill along the right bank of the Bronx.

I was charged with leading the grenadiers and light infantrymen of the left column.

The two French columns joined forces on the same road under Valentine's Hill[139]. Lauzun's Legion immediately went to the edge of Morrisania[140] in an attempt to cut the retreat of the refugees who might be there.

Fig. 4. A hussar of the Estherazy Regiment. Lauzun's hussars would have been uniformed similarly except that the coats were sky blue and the breeches chiffon yellow.

---

139   Valentine's Hill was 4 miles above Kingsbridge. 40.87820925518943, -73.87981805486099

140   Morrisania was located in what is now the South Bronx. It was on the Crown forces' route of advance to White Plains during the New York campaign and was a key point in the British lines of defense and a frequent camp site for Loyalist troops. Events at Morrisania are sometimes referred to as happening at De Lancey's Bridge, Williams's Bridge, Kingsbridge or Eastchester. 40.829320809527715, -73.90647991482304

Isnard, P.-Fr. d'. *État général des uniformes de toutes les troupes de France, représentées par un homme de chaque régiment dans le costume du nouveau règlement arrêté par le Roi pour l'habillement de ses troupes, le 21 février 1779, par M. P. F. d'Isnard,....* 1779. Strasbourg: Jean Henri Heitz, 1779. P. 181.

~~The Army~~ The American troops arriving by the Dobbs Ferry road first occupied the hills closest to Kingsbridge and some enemy outposts. The British reinforced the garrison of n° 8[141], a small fort across the Harlem River. The troops occupied all the summits around this fort. The American army took the right of the position and the French the left, occupying the forward hummocks, the grenadiers and light infantry on the most forward crests.

A battalion of grenadiers and light infantry was detached to support Lauzun's Legion. I was ordered to lead them to De Lancey's mill 3 miles on the left.

Then, the entire peninsula being occupied by troops, the enemy guards closely observed and the refugees ["repulsed" crossed out] pursued to the point and obliged to embark, the generals began their reconnaissance which was the purpose of this detachment.

They first inspected the point of Spuyten Duyvil opposite Kingsbridge from whence we can see Fort George[142], the most forward on the northernmost point of the island. From there, they followed ["from one point to" crossed out] from one hummock to another the whole length of the Harlem River as far as the tip of Morrisania, always keeping half a cannon range from the forts which had not ceased firing on the troops on the right. When they reached the very tip of Morrisania, some refugees repulsed by Lauzun's Legion, threw themselves into a house on the edge of the river and they were protected in this place by 2 pieces of cannon placed side-by-side on the island. The general's aides-de-camp

---

141 Fort no. 8 was on Fordham Heights in the West Bronx. It was larger than the other forts in the area and covered the advance of the Hessians and Lord Percy's troops during their attack on Fort Washington. 40.85603080980393, -73.90179455343437

142 Fort George was on Laurel Hill (192nd Street and Audubon Avenue on the west bank of the Harlem River, about 0.5 miles east of Fort Washington) and opposite Fort Number Eight. 40.85794532099776, -73.93173218986774

charged the refugees. The Comte de Damas[143] had a horse killed beneath him.

Our generals then returned to De Lancey's mill and from there they returned to their quarters at the rear of the army.

The battalion of grenadiers and light infantry took up its position and the troops spent the night in bivouac.

The 22 and 23 at Kingsbridge

This morning, the generals continued their reconnaissance. They went first to Frogs Neck[144]. They then followed the coast of the Sound as far the tip of Morrisania which they reconnoitered in more detail than yesterday. This point on the coast opposite Harlem is very important because, in landing a body of troops, one could capture the rear of all the works at the tip of the island.

During the generals' reconnaissance, I received the order to remain with the Chevalier de Chastellux[145] to put the troops in motion as soon as the generals issued the order. I profited by that time to go reconnoiter personally the location of the enemy works in front of our posts. I went as far as the former redoubts in front of fort n°. 8. I saw, at my leisure, the course of the Harlem River and the forts which defend it: Fort Laurel[146] opposite fort n°. 8 occupying one of the summits commanding the entire tip of the island; Fort

---

143 Charles-César d'Antigny, comte de Damas (1758-1825) was one of Rochambeau's aides-de-camp.

144 Throggs Neck (also known as Throgs Neck or Frog's Neck) is a neighborhood and peninsula in the south-eastern portion of the borough of the Bronx in New York City. It is bounded by the East River and Long Island Sound to the south and east, Westchester Creek on the west, and Baisley Avenue and the Bruckner Expressway on the north. 40.82345463397027, -73.82022530890728

145 François Jean de Beauvoir, chevalier Chastellux then marquis de (1734-1788), was a French officer, member of the Académie Française. major general in the expédition particulière. He was primarily responsible for logistics. He wrote an account of his travels Voyages de M. le Marquis de Chastellux en Amérique Septentrionale 1781, 1782, 1783 (Paris, 1786).

146 Also called Fort George. See note 69 above.

Prince Charles[147] covering the passage of Dyckman Bridge[148] where the bridge is damaged; a redoubt above Kingsbridge; Fort George at the northernmost point; Fort Knyphausen dominating the entire position on a height closer to the North River. This and Fort Laurel mutually protect each other and are linked by entrenchments and abatis[149]. We see several camps between the forts. The enemies have not ceased firing cannon shots at the curious from the various forts but they inflicted no harm.

I went with Mr. Berthier[150] to the most advanced point of Titans Hill[151] where the Americans had a very advanced post and at this point the ["which is the best at the mouth of the river" crossed out] North River winds and returns to form Harbor Creek[152] below Kingsbridge where the Spuyten Duyvil Brook empties and forms the Harlem River.

We reconnoitered Fort George very closely as well as the two frigates anchored at the tip of the island at half musket range [25-50 yards] from the shore. Independently from the military considerations, this point of Titans Hill is one of the most interesting vistas

---

147   Fort Number Nine was renamed Fort Prince Charles or the Charles Redoubt after the fall of Fort Washington on November 16, 1776. It was located below the south bank of the Harlem River on the northeast corner of Dyckman Bridge. Today, because of construction projects, it is located above the north bank of the river on Marble Hill, at Fort Charles (Corlear) Place and Kingsbridge Avenue. 40.87625043215795, -73.9095235254809. In 1779, the British constricted their outer defense line to shift manpower to other locations and many of the outposts were destroyed and abandoned. Fort Prince Charles was abandoned and destroyed by the British in 1779 as a part of this consolidation.

148   Dumas calls it Dighman's Bridge. It is sometimes called Deighton's, Dykeman's Bridge. Jacob Dyckman built the bridge in 1758 as a toll-free alternative to Kings Bridge. The stream that the bridge spanned no longer exists. See also note 75.

149   Abatis were sharpened branches pointing out from a fortification at an angle toward the enemy to slow or disrupt an assault.

150   Louis Alexandre Berthier (1753-1815) Rochambeau's aide-de-camp and cartographer. He kept journals during the American campaigns: « Journal de M. Berthier du 10 mai au 8 mars 1781 de 8 mars au 26 aout 1781 », « Campagne de mer » (décembre 1782-13 mars 1783) et « 13 mars-19 avril 1783 », published in H.C. Rice et A.S.K Brown. *The American Campaigns of Rochambeau's Army 1780-1781-1782-1783*, 2 vols. (Princeton, Princeton University Press, 1976), vol 1, 191-282.

151   Probably today's Marble Hill. 40.87609416110759, -73.91149129030701

152   40.87508911349883, -73.91543590181159

and the oddest of this region. One has no idea of the great beauty and the novelty of this landscape. Looking to the south, we see the island of New York, the course of the Harlem River and the coasts as far as Morrisania which level off all the way to the south; to the east a very wooded and hilly region, to the north the entire course of the Hudson for 30 miles, and to the west the cliffs very steep and covered with wood, sloping which enclose its bed from Dobbs Ferry, an extraordinary irregularity which has no connection with the rest of the landscape. This view of the North River is so much finer that the eye is first halted at these first sites by pointed objects and great bundles. The bed is straight for almost 15 miles as far as Dobbs Ferry. Then, it widens much and forms what is called the Tappan Sea [a line and a half crossed out] which we see in the distance. The horizon rounds out in the far distance. The mountains recede imperceptibly [illegible][153] the eye is never halted.

From the 23rd to the 24th at the Philipsburg camp

The generals, having finished their reconnaissance, ordered the retreat and the troops were set in motion in a single column at 4 o'clock. The American army forming the rearguard, I was charged with leading the artillery. We arrived at camp about midnight.

The purpose of this detachment was fully accomplished. We lost only two men who distanced themselves from the army and were killed by the refugees. We took such a position that the enemy could not send out a detachment from the island. We might have attacked fort no. 8, but it would require either having to destroy it, which would have taken the army very long, or to abandon it to the enemy again. It wasn't worth the cost.

The 25 same

---

153 Appears to read langard.

We received a more detailed report of the last affair[154] of Mr. de Lafayette against Lord Cornwallis. It appears that General Wayne got too engaged in the pursuit of the enemy rearguard. The Americans lost two cannons and captured one. Meanwhile the advantage remains uncontested with the Marquis de Lafayette because Lord Cornwallis crossed the James River and withdrew toward Portsmouth.

The 26 same

The viscount of XXX, having surrendered the position of XXX[155], I wanted to replace him, and my friends made some unsuccessful attempts to do this. However, I regarded as just and natural something that wasn't. I showed an unreasonable ambition, etc.

The 27 same

I went with Mr. de Béville to reconnoiter the communications behind the camp and the roads which were supposed to carry two columns on the other side of the Bronx to withdraw by Pines Bridge and take a position across the Croton River, a wise precaution which we did not have the time to consider until now.

---

154 The Battle of Green Spring (VA) July 6, 1781
155 Donatien-Marie-Joseph de Vimeur, vicomte de Rochambeau (1755–1813), was the son of General Rochambeau. He served as an aide-de-camp to his father and also as assistant quartermaster general. He participated in an unsuccessful campaign to re-establish French authority in Martinique and Saint Domingue in the 1790s. He was later assigned to the French Revolutionary Army in the Italian Peninsula and was appointed to the military command of the Ligurian Republic. He was appointed to lead an expeditionary force against Saint Domingue in 1802. He was captured aboard the frigate Surveillante by a British squadron at the surrender of Cap Français and returned to England as a prisoner on parole. He remained interned for almost nine years and was exchanged in 1811. He returned to the family château where he resumed the work of classifying the family's growing collection of maps which his father had begun. He resigned his place as aide to the quartermaster general of the cavalry and left the general staff of the army at this time.

We read in the *New York Gazette* that Mr. de la Motte Piquet[156] captured a merchant fleet partly loaded with plunder captured at St Eustatius.

The enemy came off the island this morning to forage 2 miles in front of Kingsbridge covered by 200 Hessian light infantrymen and 80 dragoons. We learned this from Hessian deserters who arrived during the night. We think it certain that the enemy loss on the day of the reconnaissance was 28 to 30 men.

The 28 same

It is written from Providence that our siege artillery will be loaded in a few days and ready to be transported to wherever needed and it will be there at the time Mr. de Grasse arrives. He is awaited daily.

29 same

We received news of a victory won by General Sumter's[157] troops over Lord Rawdon after which General Greene resumed the siege of Fort Ninety-Six.

Mr. de Lafayette wrote today that General Cornwallis crossed the James River and took a position and we believe he will embark troops without delay.

The 30 same

---

156   Count Toussaint-Guillaume Picquet de la Motte, also known as La Motte-Picquet (1720-1791) was a French Navy officer and admiral. He served under Louis XV and Louis XVI and took part in 34 campaigns earning the ranks of Commandeur in the Order of Saint Louis in 1780, and of Grand Cross in 1784. In 1781, he commanded a squadron of nine vessels that included three frigates. He intercepted Admiral Rodney's fleet en route from St. Eustatius which the British had captured in February 1781. He captured 26 British ships, along with Rodney's plunder in the amount of 5 million pounds sterling (about $1,281,849,640.00 in 2021).

157   Brigadier General Thomas Sumter (1734-1832) was nicknamed the "Fighting Gamecock" for his fierce fighting style against Crown forces after they burned down his house during the American War of Independence.

I went to open the communications which I reconnoitered with Mr. de Béville [line crossed out] in the rear on the left, keeping to the crests of the hills which encase the Bronx.

31 same

The same column opening continues with a detachment of 70 men.

We are assured that Lord Cornwallis and 1800 men of his army are expected at New York. A battalion of grenadiers and light infantry was brought to the rear of the left of our position and on the left bank of the Bronx. Lauzun's Legion having returned to their first camp at White Plains and General Waterbury camped 1 mile further on the left, the entire region between the Bronx and the Sound is occupied and cleared at the principal points.

I pushed the road designated for the right column as far as the road to North Castle. The more we research this region, the more we are charmed by its different vistas. Nature appears ["more" crossed out] new ["here than" crossed out] and the irregularities of the terrain are less common than everywhere else.

The French army made a general forage in the dry today 11 miles from camp on the left, very near the Sound between Rye Neck[158] and Mamaroneck[159]. It was escorted by the grenadiers and light infantry and part of Lauzun's Legion.

---

158   40.962506247765496, -73.69073765706898
159   40.94668971840986, -73.73983280801485

Fig. 5. French siege artillery at Yorktown. Translator's photo.

August

The 2 same

Nothing new for us. A few letters saying that Mr. de Grasse was anchored at Cap Français[160]. ["June 24" crossed out]. We have not received any new information from him. We hear that provisions are being gathered for the fleet at Newport.

The troops of the Pensacola garrison returned to New York 400 strong. The Spanish conditions were that these troops would withdraw to whatever place of British domination that they wanted but they could not serve there neither against Spain nor against her allies. The British, taking advantage of the fact that Spain did not recognize American independence, recalled this garrison to New York where they were put in service. The French can claim and will claim the conditions of the capitulation.

Some deserters arrive every day. A Frenchman arrived today sent as a spy and he admitted his mission and stayed in the army. It is more by vanity than by a misunderstood politic that the Americans imitate our customs and increase their luxury. We are not wise enough to completely cut back on ours. We do not incline to their customs and we do them much harm. We are unjust, ignorant decadents, impatient. They would certainly have reason to not be happy with us. A Frenchman, when he is pleased with his country, has all its prejudices and should not leave it. But, in every nation, there are a certain number of men for whom the world is their country, for

---

160 Now Cap Haitien, Haiti 19.759686989901017, -72.1957406523327

whom the different people are men among whom we find the same qualities, the same defects, the same virtues, the same vices under different forms but the same in the eye of the beholder. One prefers his own country.

One cherishes his nation, his little corner, where one has been raised and consequently where most of the ideas were gathered, but nature is the same everywhere. You have a dry heart and a poor sense if you do not admire it everywhere it appears fine.

The 3 same

I went with Mr. de Béville to examine the communication he ordered me to open 8 miles behind the camp.

["Upon coming here" crossed out] Our light troops commit heinous wrongs. They plunder several houses inhumanely. The fault of…

The 4 same

The 5 same

Two days ago, during the pleasant retreat which we made, bordering with grass the foot of several trees under which our tents were raised. We thus find ourselves in a pleasant countryside and we are rewarded with light work by the enjoyment that nature offers everywhere when we can experience it. We saw a few ships in the North River and we also observed several also going up the Sound.

The 6 same

General Washington went to reconnoiter the works around Kingsbridge this morning. The small body of light troops which escorted him went as far as the tip of Titans Hill. It is said that his Excellency went to examine suitable ground to camp the army on the other side of Valentine's Hill.

We learned from New York and we think it certain that Sir Henry Clinton[161] is returning to England and that Lord Cornwallis will become commander-in-chief. He is returning in person with 8000 men of his army. We received the same intelligence both from Virginia and from New York.

The Comte de Rochambeau went as far as New Rochelle[162] this evening to reconnoiter more closely the fleet observed in the Sound for several days. I had the honor to accompany him. We counted 30 small vessels, none of which had three masts. They were departing to the east and appeared to follow the coast of Long Island. We think these vessels are going to load forage and wood.

The 7 same

A flag of truce which brought letters for Mr. de Barras communicated the latest New York newspapers. We read the report of a ship arrived from Falmouth in 7 weeks by which it appears certain that Mr. Necker[163], Comptroller General, gave his resignation and that he is replaced by Mr. de Fleury[164]. That is said with such particular conditions that we can hardly doubt it. We hope (with the largest number of good citizens) that the newspaperman fabricated this most disagreeable news and I hope it is a well-founded lie and a new homage to Mr. Necker's glory. Nobody is personally interested that an enlightened man, just and disinterested, be at the head of finances.

Delirant reges, plectuntur achivi [Kings err; the people are punished.][165]

---

161 An unfounded rumor. General Henry Clinton (1730-1795) commander-in-chief of British forces in North America from 1778-1782.
162 40.89107577118777, -73.78578648021474
163 Jacques Necker (1732-1804) was a Genevan banker who served as finance minister for King Louis XVI between July 1777 and 1781. He took the unprecedented step in 1781 of making public the country's budget, a novelty in an absolute monarchy where the state of finances had always been kept a secret.
164 Jean-François Joly de Fleury (1718-1802)
165 Horace's Epistles 1, 14

Last night some gunboats sailed under the Dobbs Ferry battery. They were recognized as enemies and the battery fired several cannon shots at them which they returned on their return trip downriver.

British newspapers confirm the news of the capture by Mr. de la Motte Piquet.

The 8 same

It is certain that Mr. de Grasse's orders are to come here. We know he left Martinique more than six weeks ago to go to St. Domingue where he should find the Spanish.

The 9 same

The French army foraged today in front of the left at New Rochelle about 5 or 6 miles from Kingsbridge. The left of the forage was on the coast of the Sound. A great quantity of oats which was to be brought to the enemy was removed. The forage was covered by a detachment of 200 men under the orders of Mr. de Gambs[166], major of the Bourbonnais who covered the left of the forage from the sea to the Eastchester road. A mile in front of the forage, a detachment of Lauzun's Legion commanded by Mr. de Loménie[167] had occupied Eastchester since yesterday and was reinforced this morning. Finally, a battalion of grenadiers and light infantry and a cannon under the command of Mr. de la Valette[168] covered the right of the forage 1 ½ miles behind Eastchester, clearing all communication in this area and was in range to go to the part of the chain which would have been attacked. The forage was all done in the dry and

---

166 Jean-Daniel de Gambs (1744-1823) was a major in the Bourbonnais Regiment before becoming lieutenant colonel in the Royal Auvergne Regiment. He received a pension from Congress for his gallant conduct at York.
167 Dumas writes de Lomenils. François Alexandre Antoine, vicomte de Loménie (1758-1794), attaché to Lauzun's Legion.
168 Charles-François Chevalier Chaudron de la Valette (1731-) Lieutenant Colonel in the Saintonge Regiment, promoted to brigadier general for his distinguished service at the siege of Yorktown.

was done very promptly. I followed Mr. de Béville in the reconnaissance which he made in front of the forage and we returned to camp by the White Plains main road outside of the one occupied by the column of foragers.

The 10 same

I went to have a bridge repaired for the communication of the right column at North Castle and I returned by the White Plains road to examine the position of the camps which cover our left and our rear on the other side of the Bronx.

We received news from Newport about the battle of our frigates *Astree* and *Hermione* against the 26-gun frigate *Charlestown* and a 14-gun brig which escorted a convoy to Québec. Our frigates received intelligence of this convoy very late. They chased it and the enemy warships placed themselves athwart. The battle was very lively. The enemies brought their flagship after saving their convoy, but the sea was so rough that it was impossible to take possession of the 26-gun frigate. Night and a heavy fog descended and it escaped. The brig was taken and brought to Boston. Our frigates each lost about 3 men dead and 14 wounded here.

The 11 same

We learn from the New York newspapers that the 21-ship fleet captured by Mr. de la Mothe Piquet came from St. Eustatius. The news of the displacement of Mr. Necker can now hardly be believed.

Mr. de Lafayette wrote that Lord Cornwallis embarked 8000 men on 30 ships which have been stationed for several days at the entrance to the bay even though it might have profited from the favorable winds to set sail. The Marquis de Lafayette's corps is still camped at Malken Hill[169] on the left bank of the James River about 15 miles north of Williamsburg. In this position, it is in range of

---

169 The text seems to read Malken Hill but is proably Malvern Hill which is southeast of Richmond, in Henrico County, V A. 37.41144804233536, -77.2499658925777.

going to the Potomac if the enemy attempts to go back up, which is not likely, and to observe the movements at the mouth of the James and York rivers. He detached a corps under the orders of Colonel XXX[170] across the James River toward Dismal Swamp[171] to observe the enemy and to contain the parties on this side. General Wayne departed at the head of 1000 Continental troops to go join General Greene. He marched through Amelia County.

The greatest praise is given to the manner in which the Marquis de Lafayette commanded the body of American troops entrusted to him and his movements before superior forces and his extreme modesty. [Three words crossed out] This is the first time he commanded at the head and executed a campaign plan. He showed his talents ["unusual for his age" crossed out] and an experience above his age. He is spoken of very little in the French army. He is rendered curt justice.

The envious will die but never envy. The esteem of an entire nation, the glory for a European to have played a great role in this important revolution, the influence you will necessarily have in business finally the homage of all who know how to appreciate true merit will avenge him well of the unjust coldness of his compatriots.

The 12th same

Who dares have virtue in a vicious age?

Only the one who has managed to make himself independent of the others with a right heart and a strong soul, for among the most virtuous of men only a very few are found who are not slaves of some passion and who do not sacrifice their principles and their opinions. They alone depend solely on themselves. The others are

---

170 Lafayette sent Col. Josiah Parker (1751-1810) to Portsmouth, Virginia on a reconnaissance in August 1781. He found the British had embarked for Yorktown. Parker recovered 25 cannons the British had thrown into the sea to prevent their capture. David A. Clary. *Adopted Son*. Bantam Books. 2007. p. 324.

171 The Great Dismal Swamp, now a National Wildlife Refuge, is a marshy region on the coastal plain of southeastern Virginia and northeastern North Carolina between Norfolk, Virginia, and Elizabeth City, North Carolina. 36.638242347779745, -76.57477838748436

subject to those who flatter their passions and they might be corrupted by them. They cannot respond that on a given day, under certain circumstances, they will have virtue — this for....

A terrible time and after a very sad dinner, we passed a very pleasant time working ourselves to arrange our little retreat: a rock on which we piled broken trees in a picturesque manner, a very somber grotto; on the other side, a grass sofa, a few young trees which shade the base which we have cared for and surrounded with grass, a larger tree very straight covering this little refuge and interlacing its branches with the young trees whose tops barely reach the first branches. All this forms a sort of English garden made at little cost following nature and throwing away only that which detracts from enjoying its beauty. Two days of leisure sufficed with a few workers to make a very pleasant little garden out of a little corner of stony and marshy wood. It soon acquired a certain renown. The generals planned to come and we have added a little to our initial works.

The 13 same

General Washington, having dined today at Mr. de Béville's, it was proposed to him to see the camp of the assistant quartermasters general. We arranged three tables, one in front of each tent. On the first was the account and the map of the battle of Trenton. On the second, the evacuation of Boston. On the third, the junction of the French and American armies with the map of the Philipsburg camp. At the moment the general entered the little enclosure, some musicians we had hidden behind the greenery, played some marches. The general seemed moved at these honors which we heartily rendered him. He examined attentively and with the noblest modesty the different maps which seem to have been left on these tables by accident and without pretention.

The 14 same

The French army foraged again today at New Rochelle and beyond. The left of the forage was at the Sound and the right extended to the White Plains road at Eastchester. The escort was of the same strength as that of the last forage and the arrangement of the chain was about the same. We extend ourselves even more to cover the right as far as the Bronx. The battalion of grenadiers and light infantry was in reserve in this area with one field piece. All the roads ending at Eastchester were occupied by detachments of Lauzun's Legion which covered the center of the forage. The left was protected by the creek dikes which extend in the properties to the height of Eastchester and is impracticable from there to the sea. I accompanied Mr. de Béville. We first mounted the guards of the chain. We then went to reconnoiter the terrain in front and we returned to camp taking the road to the right of the forage and, passing the Bronx 3 miles from Eastchester, we followed the route of Turkey Hill[172].

A courier from Newport arrived this evening who had left on the 12th. Mr. de Barras announced, to the generals, the arrival of the frigate *Concorde* departed from Cap Français on July 28. All communication between the frigate and land was forbidden. What we have learned until now through individual letters is that the Comte de Grasse was to have left Cap Français on August 3 with 28 ships of the line and 3500 landing troops commanded by Mr. Renaud[173], Governor of St. Domingue. He was to go first to Newport and he is since awaited daily.

The confirmation of the capture of 21 ships by Mr. la Mothe Piquet who was since given 12 vessels and debarkation troops, destination unknown.

---

172 Turkey Hill/ Turkey Mountain is in Yorktown Heights, NY, west of Croton Heights, about 1.75 mi. NW of Pines Bridge. 41.24822500430773, -73.79902802923068
173 Jean-François, comte de Reynaud de Villeverd (1731-1812) served as Governor General of St. Domingue (Haiti) from May 12, 1775 - August 16, 1775 and from April 25, 1780 - July 28, 1781.

Certain news of a revolution in the East Indies and the decrease in British power on the coast of Coromandel and Malabar, the restoration of Pondicherry to the French by Hyder Ali Khan[174]

If we must believe what we have heard said today to the inhabitants who have relatives in New York and which was confirmed by the report of a prisoner, the enemies have received a reinforcement of 300 Hessians from Europe. It would require a great fund of credulity to discount.

---

174 Hyder Ali, (c. 1720 –1782) was the Sultan and de facto ruler of the Kingdom of Mysore in southern India. He concluded an alliance with the French and used the services of French workmen in raising his artillery and arsenal. He left his eldest son, Tipu Sultan, an extensive kingdom bordered by the Krishna River in the north, the Eastern Ghats in the east and the Arabian Sea in the west.

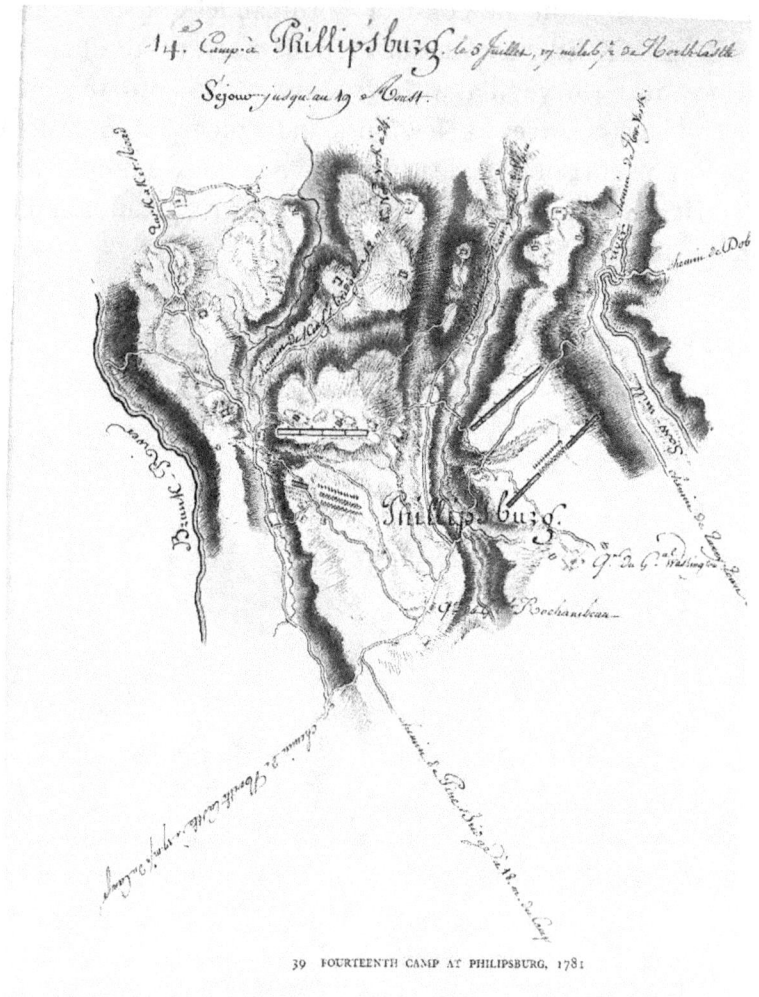

39 FOURTEENTH CAMP AT PHILIPSBURG, 1781

Fig. 6. French camp at Phillipsburg. *The American Campaigns of Rochambeau's Army*, translated and edited by Howard C. Rice and Anne S.K. Brown. Princeton, NJ: Princeton University Press, 1972. Vol. 2 #39.

The 15 same

Mr. Robert Morris[175], Minister of finance, and several other members of Congress arrived today from Philadelphia, without doubt to conduct important business with General Washington.

The certainty of the arrival of Mr. de Grasse to these shores has greatly changed politics and the politicians have reasoned in terrible form for two days. Nothing has been publicized about the details which the general received from the *Concorde,* and the decision they made after a meeting of several hours was no less secret. Mr. von Fersen was sent to Newport this morning.

Without a doubt, the arrival of a very superior French fleet in these waters would produce a happy crisis in American affairs and in ours in particular, by putting us in a state of action. And neither had the time nor the means nor the number of troops necessary to undertake the siege of New York. We can expect no good combination for the good use of the allied forces of General Washington and the Comte de Rochambeau. They had the best way of being one for the other, perfectly in agreement in mind and action. I know that I will hear it said to the contrary and each one criticized and one against the other without making a comparison between the two very different beings. I say that there is in these two souls the love of truth and goodness, the passion for glory and great talents.

The 16 same

I left camp this morning with a detachment of 30 men and 10 armed officers, 30 workers and 12 hussars. I was ordered by Mr. de Béville to survey and repair the part of Turkey Hill Road from

---

175 Robert Morris, Jr. (1734 –1806) served as a member of the Pennsylvania legislature, the Second Continental Congress, and the United States Senate, and he was a signer of the Declaration of Independence, the Articles of Confederation, and the United States Constitution. He served as the Comptroller of Finance of the United States from 1781 to 1784 and became known as the "Financier of the Revolution." He is widely regarded as one of the founders of the financial system of the United States along with Alexander Hamilton and Albert Gallatin.

the left of the camp to the base of Valentine's Hill which seems to indicate the plan to go camp in front of and as close to the enemy as possible. I had the pleasure of posting a military escort for my workers for the entire day. I only saw a very advanced American patrol which captured a few of our deserters.

17 same

It is announced that the American and French army will march continuously. We tried to make General Clinton believe that we would make another movement on Kingsbridge but our march to go to the Jerseys is arranged and set. It is now well that the French curiosity and uneasiness appear unfortunately in opposition to the discretion of the Americans which it pleases us to call unconcern. Each one makes his plan not for himself but for the others and as the Chevalier de xxx[176] says in his travels. We ask if there is any news. It was one occasion to write to Europe but I was so busy that I could not even scribble two words to my father and my uncle. I reserve for Mr. de P.[177] a reduction of all these rumors which will still be very diminished.

18 same at Drake's Tavern

The artillery received the order to leave today at noon and to go to Pines Bridge on the Croton in two marches. The army should march 1 mile to set camp at North Castle the same day.

I received the enclosed instruction from Mr. de Béville. I departed to go to Kings Ferry[178] as soon as possible. I realized that there was no other road from Pines Bridge to Kings Ferry than the

---

176 François-Jean de Beauvoir, chevalier de Chastellux (1734-1788).
177 François Jacques Chastenet, Marquis de Puységur (1716-1782). See also notes 2 and 3.
178 Kings or King's Ferry is north of Stony Point and across from Verplanck's Point. 41.24802251410307, -73.97811367003627

one through Crompond and Peekskill. I slept at Drake's tavern[179] 7 miles from Verplanck's Point.

19 North Castle

I arrived at Kings Ferry early and I enjoyed the most magnificent scene that a traveler's eye can behold. I don't know why I use the expression scene. One would have to dispel any idea of imitation, on the other hand, to recall the finest vistas, the great expanses that nature can offer in its grand and majestic proportions.

The North River, after winding through the mountains of West Point through which it seems to have opened a passage in changing its course, resumes its initial direction here and forces the latest barriers of Verplanck and Stony Point to then flow calmly into the Tappan Sea. On the Verplanck side on the left bank, the route of the mountains which enclose its bed is about 3 miles from the shore. This space is a peninsula formed by two creeks. The British occupied this post when they tried to go up the North River to join with Burgoyne's[180] army. The present fort of Verplanck is one of their works. It was repaired by the Americans. The battery is very well-placed.

I investigated the remains of the British camp and trenches and I looked for a good position for the French army to camp near the ferry. I brought to eye level the map of the region from Lents Bridge[181] on one of these creeks, of which I spoke, up to the river.

---

179   Drake's Tavern was probably along the Albany Post Road in Peekskill, NY 41.28882037689035, -73.92808338098982[?]. It was probably owned and operated by Colonel Samuel Drake of the Third Regiment of Westchester County militia. It was definitely not Joseph Drake of the 1st Regiment of Westchester County militia who lived in New Rochelle, NY.
180   Major General John Burgoyne (1732–1792) was a British general who was defeated and surrendered at Saratoga, NY. This event induced the French to support the Americans in their fight for independence.
181   Lents Bridge most likely spanned what is now called Dickey Brook which empties into Lents Cove about 1.5 miles northeast of Verplanck's Point. Lents Creek merged with Dickie Brook just before Lents Bridge and the mouth of Lents Cove on the Hudson River. 41.268385826661024, -73.93442837359461 The Lents were a prosperous family in

I retraced my steps as quickly as possible. I did not find, at Pines Bridge on the Croton River, the heavy artillery which should have arrived. The roads were so poor and so difficult that it could only get here very late and would not be in the state to cross the river the same day and to arrive at Kings Ferry in two marches according to the order of march.

I wrote to Berthier to inform him of an intermediary position between Pines Bridge and Kings Ferry and I then departed for North Castle.

I made great speed in order to be able to report to Mr. de Béville about everything I saw and especially to tell him that we do not have any boats gathered to cross the river at Kings Ferry.

I was very surprised to find nobody arrived at North Castle. I waited a long time. Finally, I learned that they had not gotten into motion until very late and that the ["the column" crossed out] field artillery was formed on this route which had just been blazed and lightly opened and which would only serve to bring the troops to the right bank of the Bronx and to take successive positions there to cover the left column which should have been the one of the baggage.

There was a terrible thunderstorm. The generals arrived tired this evening, wet and angry and I went to bed in a little corner without saying a word. I did my duty. I never had such peace of mind and such a happy heart (during the storm. I dined well with Baron de Vioménil who was wounded which prevented him from being at the brawl).

20 at Pines Bridge

The troops arrived at their camp before dawn after having passed a very difficult night. The baggage proceeded little by little. The grenadiers and light infantry under the orders of the Comte de Vioménil were ordered to form the rearguard of everything and to

---

Westchester County. The muster rolls of the Continental Army during the Revolution register the names of 28 Lents.

take the direct route to Pines Bridge where they could only arrive very late tonight. They will rest here to be able to cross the Croton tomorrow. The sun rose brighter than ever. They dried themselves a bit, quarreled, repaired and everything came to order. The Comte de Rochambeau ordered that tomorrow, the 21st, the army would camp at Hunt's Tavern which location I reconnoitered at every event and by order of Mr. de Béville.

I received an order from Mr. de Béville according to which I departed with a detachment of 60 workers to repair the roads and to precede the column to Kings Ferry.

I arrived here at night. I wrote to Mr. Berthier to inform him of the army's march and to expedite that of the artillery column to Kings Ferry. I wrote to the Chevalier de Lameth to inform him of the Comte de Rochambeau's verbal order to the Comte de Vioménil, sent by me to remain 3 miles from Pines Bridge, and to wait until the entire army and baggage had crossed the Croton to come stay at Hunt's Tavern camp tomorrow night after having passed the night here in bivouac.

21 on the Pines Bridge road at Kings Ferry

I continued to repair the roads to Hunt's Tavern where I awaited Mr. de Béville. I followed him in the reconnaissance he made of the terrain, of two positions I showed him, one on each side of the brook. He preferred the most convenient position for the troops at the foot of the valley before crossing the brook, the grenadiers and light infantry in front on the hill and the second brigade in the second line on the hill covering the brook crossing and the road by which the army would march. I already spoke of this location and I indicated it as the best on this side of the Croton.

Mr. von Fersen arrived from Newport. He brought packets to the Comte de Rochambeau and some letters from France brought to Newport by the frigate *La Magicienne*. Few people received them. A frigate departed before her, of which we have no news. It is said to have the packets for the army. It is said that the resignation of Mr.

Necker is unfortunately confirmed. We believe that Mr. de Barras's fleet was ready to set sail on the 14th.

I departed with a detachment of workers after the troops had made their camp. I worked on the roads until 9 o'clock at night. I was 8 miles from camp. I called a halt, posted my troops, made fires etc. Mr. Berthier went to report that he was very pleased to lead the artillery column to Kings Ferry in three days; that the largest part had already crossed and parked two and half miles beyond Kings Ferry in a position indicated by General Washington. Berthier returned to join me here.

22 at Kings Ferry

Two hours before daybreak, we set out to march, to arrive early at the entrance to the woods where there were very poor paths.

I followed Mr. de Béville and covered the position of Kings Ferry with him where he laid out the camp for the whole army. We then went to see his Excellency who was at Fort Verplanck. He seemed to me very tall at that moment. All our troops and part of his were engaged in battle on this exposed plateau. There was extremely quick and very focused action on the embarkation and landing. The general oversaw everything and observed attentively the course of this river for more than 25 miles, waiting to see a British frigate appear at any moment to oppose our crossing between these two points so well-known and so long contested.

I had the pleasure to go before Major Fleury[182] and after having, under a frivolous pretext, aroused his attention and fixed his attention on the other side of the river, I showed him Stony Point

---

182 François Louis Teissedre de Fleury (1749–1799), was a French volunteer and engineer captain in the Continental Army. He led one of the attacking columns at Stony Point in July 1779. Congress awarded him a medal for being the first attacker to enter the bastion and capturing the British flag. Granted leave to return to France later that year, he returned to fight at Yorktown. Back in the French army, he held commands in India and the Indian Ocean until 1790 when he returned to France. He was badly wounded early in the French Revolution and resigned. The De Fleury Medal is awarded to outstanding members of the United States Army Corps of Engineers.

where he placed the first American flag after striking the British colors. The headquarters was marked at Peekskill. The crossing of the American and French armies on the North River was done with great order and entirely thanks to the Americans who served both sides of the ferry with as much activity as intelligence. Mr. de Béville distributed the assistant quartermasters general on both sides of the river to ensure that the baggage and the troops were embarked and disembarked with order and haste. I was ordered to cross the river, to reconnoiter an emplacement for the camp of the first brigade as well as the headquarters and then to return to the ferry.

    I crossed the river in the same boat as his Excellency. This is the second time that I found myself with him on this river which he would have made forever famous by his presence. I accompanied him to his quarters two miles beyond the ferry. General Washington himself showed me the terrain where the French army would camp most conveniently 1 ½ miles from the ferry, on the side of a narrow creek on a very exposed plateau, a location both strong and pleasant. I entrusted the terrain to the brigade major and I returned to the ferry where I finished landing the rest of the artillery caissons.

Fig. 7. Artillery on carriages with caissons (lower right corner). French artillery park, Yorktown. Translator's photo.

23 at Kings Ferry

The winds having refreshed from the southwest, it was impossible to spend the rest of the night. I slept in bivouac and returned to the ferry in the morning with Colonel XX[183] who had already begun landing the caissons of the first brigade.

The campers arrived and I showed them the terrain. The Comte de Rochambeau went to West Point with General Washington – Mr. de Béville personally crossed and laid out the headquarters. He must be displeased with those who give advice, who improve everything and in whose eyes the great activity seems chaos.

24 same at the Haverstraw camp

---

[183] Anne-Alexandre-Marie-Sulpice-Joseph de Montmorency (1747-1817) was colonel of the Régiment Bourbonnais, the senior regiment of Gen. Rochambeau's army. This regiment was at the head of the first division.

Another white night. The brigade was not able to cross last night. This morning the Bourbonnais Regiment crossed and, after dinner, that of the Royal Deux Ponts[184]. The greatest part of the general staff and the wagons attached to the different parts of the administration crossed. Only the second brigade and the baggage remain on the other side.

I was relieved at the ferry by Mr. Berthier. The Chevalier de Lameth remains alone on the other side and one or the other will march with the second division.

The first [division] and the heavy artillery have orders to march tomorrow to the camp at Suffern.

I have not yet spoken about the march of the American army. After leaving the Philipsburg camp, it marched in a single column by the road along the shore of the North River, crossed the Croton at Newbridge and gained a day's march on us while we lost one in one of the defiles in the Highlands. It arrived at Kings Ferry two days before us and it crossed to camp 5 miles from the ferry on Haverstraw Heights[185] which seemed to me to be the highest crests, to close the region called the Clove[186].

The American army received the order to march tomorrow in two columns, all the troops by the closest route along the shore, called the Low Road, opening by the march of the second column

---

184 The Royal Deux-Ponts Regiment was formed in 1757 by Duke Christian IV of Pfalz- Zweibrucken as the 99th infantry regiment. The "two bridges" area (Deux-Ponts/Zweibruken) shifted over time between the French and the Germans but the regiment's loyalty always remained with France. Guillaume Christian, Comte Deux-Ponts commanded the regiment in Rochambeau's army. As English-speaking people had difficulty pronouncing French names, they did so phonetically and eventually Deux-Ponts became Dupont.

185 The camp in Haverstraw was north of Cedar Pond Brook and south of East Main St. in Stony Point Village about three miles from Kings Ferry. 41.22761167121739, -73.98272871270461

186 "The Clove was "the strategic pass starting in Suffern, New York, that led through the Ramapo Mountains, providing a back door to the important posts and Stores at West Point." It was so important that General Washington wanted it defended at all costs. Braisted, Todd. *Grand Forage 1778: The Battleground Around New York City*. Westholme Publishing, 2016. P. 127.

and blocking all the outlets along the way for three miles. This left column should be composed of one regiment of heavy artillery and baggage. It will follow the route called the High Road and will camp 3 miles ahead of the French army which will follow the same route.

Fig. 8. Uniforms of the Royal Deux-Ponts Regiment. From left to right: a fusilier, a chasseur and a grenadier.

The 25 at the camp of Suffern[187]

I resume my functions of flying deputy major aide. This morning, I reconnoitered the position of the camp in relation to the outlets to New York. I had the lodgings marked etc. I reported all this to Mr. de Béville and I then accompanied the Comte de Rochambeau on the reconnaissance he made of the area around the camp upon his arrival. This is our way of setting the positions. I reconnoiter alone first. I assure myself of the supplies and Mr. de Béville, to whom

---
187   John Suffern's Tavern was located at 110 Lafayette Ave, Suffern, NY. 41.115195928261315, -74.14994300128062

I report, corrects my ideas and presents them to the Comte de Rochambeau who decides. We camped here facing the main road obliquely, diagonally cutting the gorge in which flows a large brook. Lauzun's Legion departed to an outlet of the gorge at a fork in the roads, one of which goes to New York and the other to Pompton.

Tonight, I escaped from headquarters. I went to lodge far away. I took a bath in a clear brook. I slept in a good bed which has not happened for three days and I found the war very pleasant.

The 26 at the Pompton Meeting House camp

Same commission, same work. I traveled with great interest this morning. The hills gradually diminish at every step we make, continuing the direction of the chains to which they belong. The region opens, the cultures are more refined and the region seems more inhabited. ["The course of the" crossed out] The Pompton River waters a fertile and open field. Most of the families are of German descent. The blood is rather fine. We note a different character in the faces. It is said that there are also differences in their customs.

This people showed great indifference during this revolution — even in the very midst of the theater of war. During the first campaigns, they hardly ever took a side. They pay their taxes, hire soldiers and desire peace. The army camped in the Pompton Plains[188] behind the church.

The 27 at the Whippany camp

We continue to follow the same direction. The American army, which marches on our left, approaches closer to the North River. The advance guards are already at the Springfield location which is the strongest and closest that a body of troops can occupy on this side of the North River to clear any enemy actions on the right

---

[188] The campsite was along the Newark-Pompton Turnpike north of the Reformed Church at 529 Newark-Pompton Turnpike in Pompton Plains, 40.96458238549607, -74.29558714938146

bank of this river and to recapture those made in the Jerseys. Here at Whippany[189], we are only 18 miles from Newark.

This morning, I reconnoitered a very strong position here which the Americans occupied in the last campaigns. It is on this side of the Whippany River on a hill that dominates the entire valley and which is very steep on the front. The right of the road by which we arrive from Troy town and Percy Penny [Parsippany] and the left to the Newark road. This position is interesting because of the number of outlets which join there. We took our camp on the opposite hill across the brook. Crowning the height, Lauzun's Legion was posted on the Newark road and the advance guards extended to the bridge, 11 ½ miles from Whippany. The two divisions are to join here. Mr .de Béville had the camp of the second division marked in the second line of the first. Our march destined for Morristown after a day of rest removes any doubt that we are marching to Philadelphia and from there to Head of Elk and of our people crying: I told you so.

The 28 at Bullion's Tavern

I profited from the day of rest to gain a day ahead. I left Whippany this morning with Mr. de Béville who stopped at the village of Hanover, 2 miles from Whippany, where we were obliged to send back part of the general staff. I ran much today. I purchased a horse which I call Light. I sold another. I arrived here lightly. I advanced and prepared lodging for the Comte de Rochambeau and the Chevalier de Chastellux who are hurrying to Philadelphia. The person who suspects them the least on this route is Sir Henry Clinton. I am always enchanted by this country and its cultures and its countryside and I always hear it decried and unjustly compared to our finest provinces in Europe which have 10 times more people and many centuries of culture.

---

189 Bullion's Tavern was on Lyon's Road in Liberty Corner, Bernards, NJ 40.672873477089816, -74.5714822340077

The 29 at Somerset Courthouse[190]

I have not spoken about the location of the camp at Bullion's Tavern which the general set on the height facing the brook. Since we have taken our part, I received the order to reconnoiter the most convenient camps and to sacrifice every military advantage to the latter. Ah! What a charming view I saw today coming out of the woods, just before going down into the field where the Millstone River flows. Imagine after the detours of short but varied and enticing views, after a very somber background, a mountain full of rocks and covered with wood as old as the world, a difficult road, shaded by arches, a dark strait. All of a sudden, the veil falls. We see a very distant horizon between two trees, an elevated sky, a brilliant clarity.

Another step, the picture expands. The objects become distinct and place themselves. We discover an immense field bounded in the distance by mountains which diminish imperceptibly, the course of a fine river, roads in every direction, houses, lovely fields where such a view was never so unexpected nor has given me such pleasure.

I arrived here early. I reconnoitered the location, the placement of the camp near the church facing the river, the outlets to Brunswick etc. the position of Somerset is extremely pleasant.

The 30 at Princeton

The 31 at Trenton

---

190 Somerset Courthouse is now Millstone, NJ. It is about 8 miles west of New Brunswick and 5.5 miles south of Somerville. The site of the burned courthouse is now a private home at 13 South River Road in Millstone near the intersection of Main Street (Route 533) and Amwell Road (Route 514). South River Road intersects with Amwell Road about 100 yards east of Main Street. The site is marked by a large boulder with a bronze plaque mounted on it. 40.50223257435652, -74.58784748867014

September

September 1 – 7 at Red Lion[191]

I left Trenton at noon after having reconnoitered the ford of the Delaware under Mr. de Béville's supervision.

The 2 at Philadelphia

The 3 at Philadelphia

The 4th at Chester

This morning, the second brigade entered Philadelphia in grand parade and had the same success as the first.

I received letters from friends dated the end of April which gave me great pleasure, especially that from my brother of whom nobody had ever spoken to me. I had already closed all my letters but Jerome undertook to respond to these last ones.

I received the order to leave tonight to precede the army as usual. General Washington gave me a letter in his hand for Colonel Hollingsworth[192] at Head of Elk who will give me all the informa-

---

191 The Red Lion Tavern was on U.S. Route 13 at Poquessing Creek. 40.06483160509856, -74.98116702861964

192 Lieutenant Colonel Henry Hollingsworth (1737–1803) commanded the Elk Battalion. He was wounded in the throat by a musket ball. In 1776, he entered into a contract to furnish gun barrels and bayonets for the use of the army. He was appointed one of the superintendents for the purchase of flour, cattle, and supplies for the army in 1778.

tion necessary for the route etc. We are entering a difficult land cut by many big rivers.

This afternoon, at Philadelphia, we received almost certain intelligence from the Comte de Grasse by a small ship which spoke to a vessel having knowledge at the height of Cape Fear. The same ship said it had information about the British fleet athwart the Delaware. These reports are also confirmed by a brig which arrived here tonight.

Fig. 9. Zebulon Hollingsworth's house at Head of Elk (Elkton, MD).

The 5 at Wilmington

This city[193] is one of the finest which we have yet seen and the best situated for commerce. If a canal is ever opened from Head of Elk to one of the creeks which empty into the Delaware, the location of Wilmington will be, without a doubt, the finest in the 13 states, as it is presently one of the finest by the riches and variety of landscape.

---

193 Wilmington, DE is on the Christina and Delaware rivers. It was home to the 1802 du Pont gunpowder works and the family's Georgian-style home. 39.730475040404485, -75.53051778970277

The 5 at Wilmington

Mr. de Béville rejoined me this morning on the terrain which I was reconnoitering for a camp a mile before Chester[194] and on the right of the road. After he had determined the placement of the different corps, assigned the quarters and reviewed the itinerary which I gave him, we departed together for Wilmington. Captain Mullens[195] who was at the battle of Brandywine, showed us, along the way, the different points where the British were stopped to facilitate the retreat. We should have visited the battlefield which is more than 10 miles on the right and up the creek to get a good idea of this action. But when we consider the consequences of this defeat and we recall everything that General Washington did to repair it, we find that he is as great in his losses as in his victories.

We finally have news of Mr. de Grasse and the best ever announced in America. The entire French fleet numbering 28 ships of the line has arrived in the Chesapeake Bay. We captured a frigate at the entrance to the bay. Three vessels immediately blocked the York River. They would have gone upriver as far as the enemy position if they had had pilots. The same day the Agenois, Gatinois and Touraine regiments landed at Jamestown and joined Mr. de Lafayette's corps under the command of Major General de Saint-Simon[196].

---

194 The Blue Anchor Tavern (Fourth and Market Sts. Chester, PA. 39.81511366139345, -75.4132515899182) is one possible site where Washington and/or Rochambeau may have spent the night of September 5/6, 1781. The Pennsylvania Arms Tavern (220 Market Street, West Chester across from the Court House 39.958090022982525, -75.60759092474949) is another possible site. French forces camped along Old Chester Pike on the other side of Chester on their way south. 39.96574490607596, -75.54180092059443

195 William Mullin (Mullen) enlisted in the tenth Pennsylvania Regiment, was taken prisoner at Newark, NJ in 1780 and was exchanged at the close of the campaign of 1780 when the army was going to winter quarters. He then served in the Southern army and was present at the battle of the Green Springs [Green Springs Plantation in VA] and the siege of York. He was discharged at Philadelphia in October 1783, having served six years and eight months.

196 Claude-Anne de Rouvroy, marquis de Saint-Simon-Montbléru (1743-1819) should not be confused with his brother Claude de Rouvroy, baron de Saint-Simon (1752–1811), or his cousin, Claude-Henri de Rouvray, comte de Saint-Simon (1760–1825). He arrived at Jamestown, Virginia in late August 1781 and commanded the left wing of the allied army at

General Washington, having received the express en route, returned to bring the packets to the Comte de Rochambeau personally. He arrived here very late.

The 6 at Head of Elk

General Washington left Wilmington at dawn this morning. The encampments arrived and I indicated the reconnoitered terrain. I saw the Comte de Rochambeau and I shared his joy. This campaign should be happy. Everything is going according to plan.

I left for Head of Elk[197]. I found his Excellency here and the American army which had a march and a half ahead of us, camped a mile in front of the city on the other side of the creek. I reconnoitered a suitable emplacement to camp the French army on this side.

Mr. de Rochambeau arrived. He found two officers of Mr.de Grasse's fleet here who brought him some dispatches and who went up to Annapolis on the cutter *Le Serpent*. They confirmed verbally what we learned yesterday.

There are not enough means very near here to board the army. The grenadiers and light infantry, Lauzun's infantry, the 12-pounders and the howitzers, all under the command of the Count de Custine[198], the Duc de Lauzun, the Vicomte de Rochambeau and the Vicomte de Noailles[199].

---

the Siege of Yorktown, barring the roads toward Williamsburg and preventing the British army from escaping by land. He was shot in the leg but refused to leave the lines until the British army surrendered. He mounted his horse to take part in the surrender ceremonies.

197   Now Elkton, MD. It was called Head of Elk because it sits at the head of navigation on the Elk River which flows into the nearby Chesapeake Bay. 39.59761454323776, -75.83871458471457

198   Adam Philippe, Comte de Custine (1740 1793) was in charge of the French troops that opened the first parallel at Yorktown on October 8, 1781. He acted as a second-in-command to Claude-Anne de Rouvroy de Saint Simon.

199   Louis-Marie, Vicomte de Noailles (1756-1804) served under his brother-in-law the Marquis de Lafayette in America during the American War for Independence. He was the French officer who concluded the capitulation of Yorktown in 1781.

I was charged by the general to go reconnoiter the means to cross the Susquehanna River, and General Washington gave me a letter of recommendation which I keep as a precious title.

Some detachments of the American army also embark.

The 7 at ["Wilmington" crossed out] Head of Elk

I left very early this morning to go reconnoiter the Lower Ferry on the Susquehanna[200] and, in general, all the means to cross this river which is one of the largest on this continent.

I crossed at a small city called Charlestown[201] where we find the Chesapeake Bay. This is precisely the end of the bay and the view is fine. We see the mouth of the Susquehanna and opposite the Eastern shore which is a more fertile land than this side of the coast. Charlestown is very well-placed for commerce. The city will be one of the last to increase in size but it will become large because of the population of the two states of Pennsylvania and Maryland and the relation that will exist between them. It is better placed than Head of Elk where ships of a little strength cannot ascend.

The shores of the Susquehanna are not pretty in this area. The riverbed is not deep but the lands are poor and little cultivated.

I charged a man named Captain Chest[202] to go get information about the ford which is 18 or 20 miles above this ferry (see the reconnaissance of the river).

Upon my return, I went to report to Mr. de Béville and then to his Excellency and to the Comte de Rochambeau. I proposed to march the army in two columns. The left one composed only of the infantry unencumbered by any type of baggage, should cross

---

200 Susquehanna Lower Ferry is now known as Havre de Grace, Maryland. People arrived via the Post Road, the major north/south route of travel. They stayed at the taverns and crossed the Susquehanna River on one of the ferries. 39.5524749518552, -76.0909500034244 Colonel John Rodgers Tavern on the other side of the Susquehanna River was also known as Lower Ferry. The location became Perryville (after Mary Perry, wife of John Bateman) when it incorporated in 1882. 39.55720659186054, -76.07804321210519
201 Charlestown, MD 39.57472556583499, -75.97566343840917
202 John Chace or Chase?

at Lower Ferry and the right column, composed of all of Lauzun's Legion, the field and park artillery and the baggage will cross at the ford of Bald Friar's Ferry[203] and rejoin the left column at Bushtown[204]. We await receipt of the report of the man I sent to reconnoiter the ford to decide this march.

The 8 at Head of Elk

General Washington left this morning with very little entourage to go to Baltimore and from there by land and with the greatest haste to Williamsburg. He should, in passing, see his house on the Potomac. This will be the first time since the beginning of the war.

The Comte de Rochambeau and the Chevalier de Chastellux left a few hours after his Excellency. Our general left the Baron de Vxx[205] precise instructions on the army's march.

The 8 at Bric's[206] meetinghouse

---

203   Bald Friar Ford and Ferry is said to have been kept by a bald-headed man named Fry and was named after him. George Johnston, History of Cecil County (Elkton, 1881), p. 345. The ford is 2 1/4 miles wide, 7 miles upstream from the present Conowingo Dam. This was the only one practicable, but barely so, since the bottom was so rocky that the horses risked breaking their legs. 39.70482545436607, -76.2129786475943

204   Bushtown or Bush Town was officially known as "Harford Town" since 1774 but the contemporary French campsite maps refer to it as Bushtown. It was located at the head of the Bush River between present-day Joppa and Aberdeen. 39.47261652517281, -76.27010476109906.

205   VioméniI

206   The text appears to read Bric's or Brie's. The name does not appear in any of the known diaries or on any map. The artillery, wagons (305 wagons drawn by more than 1,800 animals), another 1,500 horses (for officers and the Auxonne artillery), and Lauzun's cavalry (400 men and horses) under the command of René-Marie vicomte d'Arrot crossed the Susquehanna at Bald Friar's Ferry. Jean-François-Louis, comte de Clermont-Crèvecoeur makes no mention of where he lodged that night.   Marie-François Joseph Maxime, Comte de Cromot Du Bourg and Ludwig Baron von Closen both spent the night at Porter's Mill on Octoraro Creek while the troops camped at Cumming's Tavern on the east bank of the Susquehanna River. Daniel Friedrich Sotzmann's map, *Maryland und Delaware* (Hamburg, 1797) shows Porter's Mill about 2 miles east of the river bank and an unnamed meeting house about two miles east of Porter's Mill. That is likely where Dumas lodged. The map shows another meeting house (Cookson's?) about 5 miles further east.

On the road to Bald Friar's Ferry

Having received the enclosed reports this morning, in response to the instruction I gave to Captain Chew, I halted the itineraries of the two columns and I dressed the order of march in two columns to cross the Susquehanna which the generals decided to do yesterday. Mr. de Béville approved and corrected it. I was charged to lead the right column. See the pieces related to this. [not included in the draft]

I also received a personal instruction according to which I departed this evening with a detachment of workers to survey and repair the roads by which the right column would march. I was delayed. Night overtook me *en route* and I had the detachment halt in a barn.

The 9 on the right bank of the Susquehanna

I set out to march at dawn and I arrived at the Octoraro[207] early which I forded. This part is sparsely habited and the land is sandy, clay and of poor quality. But the rustic and almost wild regions are still pleasant by their variety.

Arrived on the Octoraro, I did not find Colonel Wadsworth and the other people charged with the supplies at the agreed-upon location. I went to reconnoiter, a mile beyond, an emplacement for Lauzun's Legion. I met these men a few minutes later. They assured me that the army's baggage could not arrive any closer than 8 miles from Bald Friar's Ferry because of the lack of fields in this entire region. I returned on the Octoraro where Mr. Berthier did not hesitate to join me. I handed him the attached letter which I just wrote to him and communicated to him Colonel Wadsworth's note

---

207 Octoraro Creek is a 22.1-mile-long (35.6 km) tributary of the Susquehanna River, joining it 9 miles (14 km) above the Susquehanna's mouth at the Chesapeake Bay. 39.66698356356175, -76.14813319568474

which authorized me to change the march of part of the column. He departed to halt it at Cummings Tavern[208].

Mr. de la Valette informed me that he had been charged to lead all the army officers across the ford of the Susquehanna and that they should follow the marches of the rest of the column. I engaged him to have them cross the river today and I assigned quarters to the various regiments. I then gave Mr. Sheldon a list of the quarters on the Octoraro and I went to the ferry. [Two words crossed out] All the line officers crossed the ford under my supervision without accident. I assigned guides to each group and I remained at the ferry to see the first wagons cross.

I received a letter from Mr. de Béville which ordered me to have all the trains of soldiers cross first. I had already taken the precaution to have them advance as far as the Legion's camp. I wrote and addressed to Misters Berthier and Sheldon the following day's itinerary and I crossed the river at the same time as the comptroller's six wagons were crossing the ford. I was happy with this attempt.

I must here explain a funny sketch to the pleasant story of the ford and the falls of the Susquehanna. It's usually at the edge of the rivers that we find extraordinary scenes. It is fordable everywhere. There are falls or cascades not very ["these places were" crossed out] high but very attractive along the whole width of the river about 50 toises[209] below the ford. The bed is enclosed by wooded mountains. Their cut is bizarre. The rocks, the trees bending on the shores show that one cannot ascend the river this far. As soon as we spot a few houses on the shore, we barely find the trace of man and the effects of his destructive hand. It is an odd thing to see a column of cavalry cross directly across the river without danger despite the rapid currents and the thundering of the falls. On the right bank, the scene is not great but more pleasant. An infinity of little islands covered with trees with the finest foliage of which a few almost form

---

208 Battle Swamp east of the Susquehanna and after the crossing by Bald Friar Ford at Deer Creek Friends Meeting. 39.64643052632224, -76.20513806572669
209 A toise is an old type of French measurement. It is equal to 1.949m. So 50 toises would be 97.5m or 106.5 yards.

a canopy[210] and cover the rapid and foaming current which escapes the cascades. We would think we were separated from these pretty little islands by an obstacle so difficult to cross that we are very surprised to approach it on horseback everywhere. The people who are in pirogues[211] and who go very quickly see the bottom of the water everywhere and can even touch it. Finally, I have not yet seen ["such fine" crossed out] landscape more pleasant than this part of the Susquehanna River.

However, I was detained longer than I would have liked. The detachment of workers which I sent to repair the passage by which the wagons were to come out of the ford made a mistake and repaired another and we had to spend the whole night working on this passage.

The 10th at the Bushtown camp

Lauzun's Legion began to cross the ford at dawn. When I saw it completely on the other side safely, along with the wagons of tents, I went ahead to mark the camp of the artillery and the army's baggage at Deer Creek Church[212]. Lauzun's Legion had taken a wrong turn. I put it on the right road and, after having already reconnoitered the camp 8 miles from Bald Friar's Ferry, I returned to the head of the column. Mr. de xxx had taken a different road than the one I indicated. His example led the people charged with supplying the column to the point that I would indicate and the forage etc. was prepared 3 miles from the camp which I had marked. I met Berthier to whom I reported all this. I ran to the place which had been supplied. Finally, before the head of the artillery column arrived, everything was supplied. They gave me a satisfactory report of crossing the ford with few almost inevitable breakdowns.

---

210 Dumas uses the word which translates as "cradle."
211 Pirogue is a flat-bottomed boat six to 20 feet long with flaring sides and a sharp bow used for fishing and transportation in swamps and bayous. Propelled by paddles or poles.
212 Deer Creek Friends Meeting. 39.64643052632224, -76.20513806572669

I went to Bushtown to report to Mr. de Béville about the right column's crossing of the Susquehanna.

He had just left for Baltimore ["I [illegible verb] crossed out] I went to report to the Baron de Vioménil. My report relieved their minds a bit. We feared the crossing of this column at the Susquehanna ford. The officers who had all arrived without the least accident believed or said they had arrived by miracle. They had taken a wrong road and they were wagering that not a single baggage wagon would arrive. I have a lot to respond, to refute. I could only satisfy the reasonable people. I withdrew very tired in any case.

The 11 at Baltimore

The army which had come to Bushtown from Head of Elk in two marches, after crossing the Susquehanna at Lower Ferry continued to march this morning to camp at Whitemarsh[213] 15 miles from Bushtown and 11 from Baltimore. Consequently, the baggage column, which had 16 miles more to make because of the detour at the ford, remained one day's march behind. The general sent me an open letter this morning in response to that of Mr.de la Valette who informed him of some damages to some wagons and that it was impossible to rejoin the army the same day. I was very interested to see this column in motion with my own eyes. I took a relay and went to the camp at Deer Creek. I found the artillery en route and all the baggage wagons which were parked a mile behind the artillery. I met Mr. Berthier who reassured me very much and soon after the Chevalier de la Valette who handed me a letter for the general and who wrote me a ticket explaining the state of the baggage column. I put this ticket in order this evening.

I recrossed at Bushtown. From there, I went to Little Falls[214] to lay out a plot for the artillery. This part of Maryland is not good and

---

213 Whitemarsh is about 10 miles northeast of Baltimore, MD. 39.37267103047805, -76.46126003781245
214 Little Fall was in the area near where I-95 crosses the Big Gunpowder Falls River in White Marsh, MD. 39.38518665334353, -76.4415634220172

consequently less inhabited than the other states. We hardly ever leave the woods. We find a few large houses here and there, but we notice that the region is little inhabited. On the other hand, I am not bored with seeing woods in this season and I surprise myself saying despite myself: What a fine country when I see many trees. I love trees. I was admiring this morning a corner of forest where lightning damaged, split or denuded some superb oaks a short while ago.

From Little Falls where the little cascades, which are several mills one above the other and form, in effect, very fine cascades, I went to the Whitemarsh camp where the Marquis de Laval[215] commanded in the absence of the brother generals who went to expedite the preparation of the ships destined to embark the army at Baltimore. I stopped only long enough to make a report. I wanted to arrive at Baltimore despite the poor roads, the rain and the thunderstorm and the darkest night in the midst of the woods. A Quaker who was traveling alongside me for a quarter of an hour, without either of us doubting the other, served as my guide and his conversation and questions about the French army made the road seem very short. I arrived at Baltimore where everyone was asleep. I handed over the letters with which I was charged. I met my brother by sheer luck in the middle of a street. At the time, I was very embarrassed to find Mr. de Béville's lodging. This encounter consoled me for the adversities of the day but not my horses for the 40 miles they traveled.

The 12 at Baltimore

This morning I saw Mr. de Béville to whom I reported in great detail about the mission he entrusted to me. I saw the city which is very fine, very lively, newly constructed and which will one day be as famous for her trade as for the pleasure and advantages of its location. It is laid out in a line. The main street, more than ½ a mile long, is the finest possible. The creek on which or around which

---

215 Anne Alexandre Marie Sulpice Joseph de Montmorency, marquis de Laval (1747-1817), French general commanding the Bourbonnais Regiment.

Baltimore was built does not go any higher than this valley. We count 4 or 5 miles from the point where the streets are at the mouth of the creek in the Chesapeake Bay and it widens more and more approaching the bay. The frigates cannot ascend this river, but ships of 300 tons can come alongside the streets.

We found here only insufficient means to embark the French Army. Whatever activity, whatever efforts we put into this research, we cannot flatter ourselves for being able to embark the entire first brigade comprising the individuals, the baggage, the indispensable and necessary munitions of war and of mouth. This is only for the remainder, an overview according to D., my friend whose general particularly charged him with making this reconnaissance and who did it well. Mr. de Béville, whom this work particularly concerns, is taking care of it at this moment.

The Army arrived as well as the artillery park. The first brigade is camped on this side of the city near the embarkation points and the second [brigade] on the other side as well as Lauzun's Legion and the park.

The 13 at Baltimore

I and all the other assistant quartermasters general received an instruction this morning from Mr. de Béville to inspect the streets and ships destined to transport the troops. We were much further ahead than that, as we tried to embark, but this attempt was suspended. Mr. de Béville's instruction is well done and should serve as a model. I am angry that it was not disseminated more widely. Mr. de Béville had barely gathered the reports which we gave him and put in order the general state of the means of embarkation than the general decided we would march by land, that as much baggage as possible would be loaded so as to lighten the wagons and that the entire army would march by land.

Mr. de Béville had already taken all the necessary information for the march of the baggage column. He immediately prepared two different orders of march: one for the Legion which leaves tomorrow, 14, and should march for long days, and Mr. Sheldon is charged with leading it and another for the army which will depart on the morning of the 16th. These different parts are included in the general instruction for the route and particularly for the crossing of the Potomac River which Mr. de Béville transmitted to me this evening. I resume my functions. I am charged with the preliminary reconnaissance and I am very pleased with the way I am employed.

Now, we could embark 1000 men and, if the same supposition continues, the same station of our fleet, the same immediate need of land troops, it seems that we should embark them. Did the general decide only on the impossibility proven and re-proven of embarking more than a thousand men? I think not. He has orders or other reasons.

We disseminate, we even print in public newspapers that Mr. the Comte de Grasse went out and that he had an engagement with Admiral Hood[216] who was, it is said, at our total advantage. There is no official report yet.

Before leaving Baltimore, a brief word about the women as I speak constantly about the trees [one word crossed out]. They are generally not pretty. This evening, I saw a rather large gathering at Mr. Smith's and there were only one or two people of note. They comported themselves ridiculously. They seemed flirtatious and unpleasant to me. I agree that this judgment is severe, especially on the part of someone who only saw them. There are many French settled here and French is spoken more than in any other city in America. There are also many Tories.

The 14 at Mr. Jones's plantation
on the road to Georgetown

---

216 Admiral Samuel first Viscount Hood (1724-1816) joined Admiral Thomas Graves (ca. 1725-1802) in the unsuccessful effort to relieve the army at Yorktown when Admiral, the Comte de Grasse drove off the British fleet in the Battle of the Chesapeake.

I left at dawn this morning with the Legion camp. I stopped at Elk Ridge Landing[217] to examine the ferry and the ford on the Patapsco. I reported immediately to Mr. de Béville about this (see the related pieces[218]) and especially the itineraries which I send regularly and in which I include all my remarks on the terrain. I then went to Spurrier's Tavern[219] where, after inspecting a camp for the army 1 mile to the east, I sent another dispatch.

Finally, after having wandered about, I came to sleep here on the ground where the army should camp on the second march leaving Baltimore. I am at a farmer's, a very good man, a good Whig who has never been more than 10 miles from his plantation. I saw his entire family occupied spinning wool. Since the beginning of the war, this whole lower region of Maryland can no longer conduct foreign trade in tobacco and receive manufactured goods in exchange. The settler is obliged to make the cloth to clothe himself. He never tried it, but he experienced that he can satisfy himself. The lands are poor and sandy in his entire region and it is less cultivated than the others and less inhabited. We harvest only what is absolutely necessary to survive. There are few cattle. Going to the north, we find a land little inhabited, excellent land, a people devoted to farming, but very little trade which exchanges surplus, produce for cloth and commodities. Thus, this region has suffered little and that of the coast and between the navigable rivers is absolutely ruined.

The 15 at Alexandria

This morning I inspected a plot suitable to camp beneath Willet's Tavern with the Piney Branch Brook[220] in front of it. I wrote to Mr. de Béville, sent the itinerary from Willet's Tavern to Georgetown

---

217 Elkridge Landing was a Patapsco River seaport in Maryland and is now part of Elkridge, Maryland. 39.21808529680001, -76.70642221262658
218 These pieces became separated from this manuscript.
219 Dumas refers to it as Superior's Tavern. Spurrier's Tavern was near present Waterloo at the intersection of MD-SR 175 and US 1. 39.17197951013343, -76.78590143010187
220 Piney Run or Creek is located in Alexandria, VA. 38.760838767231554, -77.13829634130057

where I went to learn about the means that were gathered to cross the Potomac River. I saw Lauzun's Legion and the artillery horses cross. I came to sleep at Alexandria where Colonel Euverie[221], Governor General, Master of the state of Virginia, handed me the state of the boats which remained in Alexandria. I learned from him that the Baron de Vioménil had asked him for information about the Alexandria Ferry because he counted on crossing by the most direct route to Bladensburg[222] at this city, while the baggage column would pass by the Georgetown Ferry. This arrangement being contrary to the instructions which I received from Mr. de Béville, I wrote to him sending him the state of the assembled boats here and at Georgetown and the itinerary from Bladensburg to here.

The news of the engagement of the Comte de Grasse with the British is certain. It is confirmed in a personal letter to the Marquis de Lafayette, but we do not yet have an official account of this action.

The grenadiers and light infantry embarked at Head of Elk received the order to put into port at Annapolis until further order. Mr. de Grasse, having gone out of the bay, it was possible that a small British ship, hidden in a cove, might intercept this fleet, and our generals did not want to even risk this chance against the success of the expedition.

Going through Georgetown, I saw a regiment of 400 men, newly recruited, well-armed, well-dressed. This is the second which the state of Maryland sends to the Marquis de Lafayette's army. These troops were at the High Spirits for 15 days. The states of Maryland and Virginia are making the greatest efforts. The presence of General Washington who is coming personally to defend his country certainly contributes much.

---

221 Unknown person. Thomas Jefferson was governor of Virginia from June 1, 1779 to June 3, 1781. He was succeeded by William Fleming June 3-12, 1781 and Thomas Nelson Jr. June 12-Nov. 22, 1781.

222 Bladensburg, MD was a seaport town during the colonial period. It became a designated tobacco inspection and grading port. Its role as a seaport faded as the Anacostia River silted up and larger ships could no longer reach the port. However, the town remained an important crossroads of routes north to Baltimore and Philadelphia, south and east to the towns of Annapolis and Upper Marlboro. 38.942240105211376, -76.94388941264162

The Potomac separates Maryland and Virginia. General Washington's house[223] and lands are 8 miles from Alexandria, on the right bank of the Potomac. I hope to visit the home of this great man. We cannot hear speak of him to his fellow citizens without being filled with respect and attachment to his person as they are. There is not a single Tory in the city and all the others are filled. He arrived the other day to stay at home. As he was unannounced, Mrs. Washington[224] sought to guess what officer was crossing the Potomac alone in a boat opposite his house. As soon as he set foot on shore, he was surrounded by the Negroes of his plantation who prostrated themselves and kissed his feet. More than 1000 militiamen took up arms and vowed to not leave him. He had much difficulty in convincing them that their help was not needed by the army at this time and that he would call them when the time was right. He ordered them to repair the road and they effectively worked on it very much. General Washington spent two days at his house. He saw arrive the Comte de Rochambeau and the Chevalier Chastellux who followed him very closely and he departed for Williamsburg. It is said that the joint corps of the Marquis de Lafayette and that of Mr. de Saint-Simon are about 12 miles from the enemy, that Lord Cornwallis works at increasing his means of defense and that he expelled all the useless mouths from his location.

The 16 Georgetown

I returned here to wait for Mr. de Béville according to his instructions.

We received at Annapolis and sent to the army the confirmation of the victory won by our fleet on that of the English. While waiting for the report, authentic reports arrived that the British were cruising in the cape wind while Mr. de Barras was to the south trying to enter the bay. He had his light ships signal those of Mr. de Grasse

---

223   George Washington's home is at 3200 Mount Vernon Memorial Hwy, Mt Vernon, VA. 38.71009843575336, -77.08773088973166
224   Martha Custis Washington (1732-1802),

that he had had knowledge of the enemy. Mr. de Grasse went out with 21 ships, gave chase to the British. These formed their line of battle, and Mr. de Barras, having rallied the fleet, chased the British away. Mr. de Grasse pursued them. He took the 44-gun *Roebuck*. The frigate *Ruby* and 2 transports with troops. Mr. de Grasse reentered the bay with all his forces consisting of 37 ships of the line. It is said we are sending transport vessels [to] Annapolis to take the troops. I fear that the commission with which I am honoured will make me the last to arrive. I will be left here for the baggage and all the troops will march to Annapolis to board there.

The 17th in Alexandria

I waited in vain for Mr. de Béville. It has been rumored that the French army had received orders at Spurrier's Tavern and that it would march to Annapolis to be embarked there along with the baggage. I received a letter from Mr. de Béville, after having spent the day in the uncertainty of staying with the baggage, that I always assumed would come to Georgetown. The general recalls me to Annapolis. I left a letter with itineraries, the state of the boats, etc. at Georgetown for the officer in charge of conducting the baggage. I came here where I first rented some horses and a guide to go to Annapolis tomorrow. I send my horses [a line and a half crossed out] by land with the baggage of the American army which passes through here tomorrow morning, and I will arrive at Annapolis alone, very happy to have escaped the tiring and detested chore at this time to conduct the army's baggage.

The 18th in Annapolis

I arrived here a few hours after the troops who camped last night at Scot's House[225] 6 miles from Annapolis. The baggage column

---

225 Scott's Plantation was known as Belvoir. It was at 1487 Generals Hwy, Crownsville, MD 21032, about 7 miles from the center of Annapolis. 39.016093884818545, -76.58157895232421

did not continue to march to Georgetown because we think that there will be enough room to embark everything and the Baron de Vioménil ordered everything to go to Annapolis.

The transport ships that have ascended this far are the same as those that Mr. de Barras conveyed from Rhode Island. They are escorted by *Le Romulus* and the frigates *L'Aigrette*, *La Diligente*, *La Gentille*, *Le Richemond* and *L'Iris*. The latter two were taken at the offing of the capes by the French frigates when Mr. de Grasse returned to the bay after his battle. They had been sent to cut the buoys, which they had largely executed. They were forced to indicate the locations of the anchors but several of them have been lost. Lord Rawdon was put on board the frigate *La Diligente* where he is treated with great respect. The Americans who blame him for atrocities wish we were less generous.

Fig. 10. The French camp site at Scott's Plantation. Photo courtesy of Dr. Robert A. Selig.

The country I crossed today between the Potomac and Annapolis is neither beautiful nor good. The land is sandy and almost all covered with wood. However, I have seen large dwellings around the small town of Marlboro[226]. A lot of tobacco is harvested there.

The 19 in Annapolis

Mr de Béville, having surveyed the encampments alongside the king's ships and transports, determined the distribution of troops and effects. I was in charge of the embarkation of the artillery, provisions and hospitals. Today, we embarked the effects of the regiments and some horses (because the general promised that he would embark 50).

Annapolis is a pretty little town, pleasantly located on a hill in the end of a cove where the anchorage is good for the largest merchant ships. There are many beautiful houses, a state house, a remarkable building by the elegance of its [one word crossed out] interior decoration. As these happy beginnings are due only to trade, they were interrupted by the war and this city, drawn on a rather extensive plan, has not a street where the houses [are] contiguous.

The blood is quite beautiful here. I saw some pretty women. A Mrs. Lloyd[227], who can be noted as one of the most beautiful women in America. She was raised in England, and then in Paris. She speaks French. She is perfectly at ease. She has all the manners of our little mistresses, [and] she has a very jealous husband. All this had great success for the army. I find her very beautiful. Mrs. Stone is ["very"? crossed out] pretty, very well made, very happy and very lovable.

---

226 Written as Malborough. Marlboro, MD is east of Alexandria, VA. 38.82063925509401, -76.74708458361404

227 Joanna Leigh Lloyd (1758-1814) and her four sisters inherited the fortune of the rich merchant John Leigh of Northcourt House, Isle of Wight. She married Richard Bennett Lloyd (1750-1787) in 1775. Mr. Lloyd was an ensign in the 2nd Regiment of Foot Guards (Coldstream Guards) from 1773 to 1775. Louis François Bertrand Dupont d'Aubevoye Comte de Lauberdière and Baron Ludwig von Closen concur with Dumas. See *The Road to Yorktown: The French Campaigns in the American Revolution, 1780-1783.* Edited by Norman Desmarais. El Dorado Hills, CA: Savas Beatie, 2020. p. 217 and Closen, Ludwig, Baron von. *Revolutionary Journal 1780-1783*, translated and edited with an introduction by Evelyn A. Acomb, Chapel Hill, N.C.: University of North Carolina Press, 1958. p. 220.

Fig. 11. Joanna Lloyd and Richard Bennett Lloyd painted by Henry Benbridge ca. 1782. Private collection.

The 20 in Annapolis

We continue to embark the various effects of the army. The Comte de Fersen returned to carry a letter from the Comte de Rochambeau who hastens the embarkation of the troops. Whatever energy is exerted, the convoy ships are already so loaded that it is very difficult to load all the baggage and subsistence of the army. It might have been better to let the baggage column go by land as it did at Spurrier's Tavern. We could have embarked the troops here with greater speed and we certainly would have gained a few days. The empty wagons can only leave here after tomorrow and will not arrive in Williamsburg until October 6. Sic volvere[228]—

The 21st aboard the frigate L'Aigrette

---

228 So be it

The troops were embarked this morning from 7 o'clock until noon. The convoy, which was anchored off the points, the cove, set sail to join the king's ships which are still anchored offshore. At 5 o'clock, the winds were at the N.N.E. good fresh. We set sail.

Approaching the mouth of the Patuxent where navigation is more difficult, we signaled to anchor.

So here, the French and American armies are very close to joining the corps of the Marquis de Lafayette after a 33-day march made with order and speed during which everything was planned both for the troop movements, for subsistence, almost no sick, strict and well-maintained discipline, finally all our means of siege, all our ammunition of war and mouth transported to the point where we want to operate. Whatever the fate of the weapons and the promptness and the difficulty of success, we will owe it to the wise combinations, to the accuracy and good plans of the Comte de Rochambeau for having led this expedition with a rare agreement, especially in a country like this.

The 22 on board *L'Aigrette*

We had as good weather as possible. The entire day was devoted to examining the coasts of the Chesapeake Bay which we never lose sight of. The bay is only 25 miles wide at its greatest width. We have successively recognized the mouths of the Potomac, the Rappahannock and other rivers that flow into the bay. This cruise is the most pleasant imaginable, but as we were occupied with the position of Lord Cornwallis, of the anchorages of our ships at the mouth of the York River, that we were impatient to find the Comte de Grasse's fleet, we admired little, we little enjoyed these great beauties of nature. Thus, the turn of ideas is most often the principle of our affections. I embarked with Mr. de Béville and Chevalier de Lameth from whom I rarely separate and never without difficulty. Around 5 o'clock in the evening, we were across the York River where 4 ships of the line are anchored. The Chevalier De Cambis[229], in command of *L'Aigrette* received an order from Mr. de Villebrune, captain of the *Romulus*[230] to crowd the sails to go and report to Mr. de Grasse of the arrival of the convoy from Annapolis. We anchored in the middle of the navy on a dark night that did not allow us to distinguish anything but the commander's lights.

The 23rd aboard the *Romulus*

The Chevalier de Cambis having been ordered to anchor with his frigate opposite Hampton Bay, we set sail in the night to go up the James River. We barely spotted the navy at dawn. We anchored at the appointed place. We put our belongings in a rowboat and we all, General Béville's family, went to request asylum aboard the *Romulus*. This little campaign was upsetting. We were received politely and after having distributed on board two other frigates the companies of the Royal-Deux-Ponts which were on board the *Aigrette*, it was decided that we would be allowed to stay aboard the *Romulus* where de Vioménil's generals were. No sooner were we on board, than the ship, driven by the currents, approached the frigate *L'Aigrette* which we had just left and which was at anchor in the channel. I would say to you, like this other, Madam, you may never have been boarded.

It's a terrible shock, a crash, the front ends swept away. The bravest sailors fleeing to the other end of the bridge and the two ships taken and lashed by the maneuvers so that we ["both"? crossed out] don't understand anything and everyone screams during this pleasant [sic] event. The frigate *Le Richemond* which followed the *Romulus* was also dragged and came alongside the two ships already approached. New screams, new embarrassment. Finally,

---

229 Joseph de Cambis vicomte de Cambis (1748-1825) commanded *L'Aigrette* from 1781 to 1783. He captured the British brig *Tarleton* off the island of Aix on March 22, 1782.

230 The French navy captured the 44-gun HMS *Romulus* in the Chesapeake Bay and took her into service as *Le Romulus* under the command of Lieutenant de Vaisseau Jacques-Aime Le Saige Chevalier de la Villebrune. She ferried troops to Annapolis for the Siege of Yorktown.

we managed break free, but we had another diversion the same evening. During supper, someone whispered in our ear that there was fire on board. We continued to eat briefly but without appetite. The fire had spread to the kitchens and those who knew that the ship was trimmed English-style carried some of its powder to the front and amused themselves a little with the noise of the pumps that lasted until midnight.

24 in Williamsburg

The Romulus ran aground and the pilots despaired refloating her with the tide. They decided to request help from boats transporting the troops who were on board. Mr. de Béville took charge of this duty. We reboarded our rowboat loaded with effects and tried to go up the river. This rowboat drew 3 feet of water. Our pilot sank us in the midst of the sandbars in Warwick Bay[231]. We had great difficulty finding the channel. During that time, the convoy set sail. A ship took us in tow. Finally, we arrived at Williamsburg Creek[232] at nightfall, where we found many American ships landing troops and effects. We went back up the creek with great difficulty and after finally disembarking at College Landing[233], we arrived at Williamsburg, in the dwelling of the Comte de Rochambeau. One of the Baron of Vioménil's aides-de-camp had preceded us there and had announced to the general that *Le Romulus* had been refloated and that the whole army was coming. After taking orders from the general, we went to see the general the Marquis de Lafayette who will have his share of glory in this matter and which is in a charming way for the French. Everyone is delighted to see him. Here, he has no rivals and the envious do not dare to appear so [one word crossed out].

---

231 Dumas is probably referring to the bend in the James River near the mouth of College Creek. 37.22054518361693, -76.69342811795609
232 This is probably College Creek, south of the city. 37.219588304180796, -76.70836265694362
233 37.25149594193023, -76.7102540572552

The 25 in Williamsburg

The general gave his orders for the landing of the troops, the field artillery and the baggage. They landed successively and camped near the landing beach at the entrance to the creek, 6 miles from Williamsburg. The assistant quartermasters general were successively used there. I returned to Williamsburg to mark the headquarters, etc.

Before the American and French troops who are arriving from the north are fully reunited with the Marquis de Lafayette's corps and that of Mr. de Saint-Simon, I reconnoitered the position that the latter occupied, a position that will become interesting if Lord Cornwallis's army capitulates and he is unfairly reproached for not having tried to fight a battle before the arrival of Generals Washington and Rochambeau. In front of the city of Williamsburg and on the left, there is a deep ravine whose origin is very close to the Yorktown Road. Thus, this ravine, that goes as far as the York River, covers and envelops this left side. To the right of the land beyond the road and opposite this ravine is a beautiful field open to the James River. Behind this right is the city and College Creek which flows into the James River after a course of 6 miles. It's behind the city and the creek that the Marquis de Lafayette took his position, with his battlefield in front of his right. He had stationed a light infantry corps on the edge of the ravine in front of the city on the left, and the riflemen corps under General Muhlenberg[234] was stationed in the woods two miles ahead of him, occupying the main outlets on York and the rivers. Mr. de Saint-Simon had [one word crossed out] strengthened this position by camping his troops to the left of those of the Marquis de Lafayette. The grenadiers and

---

234 Brigadier General John Peter Gabriel Muhlenberg (1746–1807) was a Lutheran minister who served in the Continental Army. He commanded the first brigade in Lafayette's Light Division at the siege of Yorktown,

light infantry and the detachment under the command of Mr. de Choisy[235] occupied the plateau below the ravine in front of the city.

This position is such that it could not be turned. The enemy could not force the Marquis de Lafayette to abandon it by any movement. This was to warn him of any river crossings and Lord Cornwallis would naturally have to wait for help because it was not likely that he would abandon the position and the York works.

The 26th in Williamsburg

I went to the landing site this morning. All the troops had landed. We continued to disembark the baggage. The lack of wagons delayed us a lot. The Americans, who have a larger number of harnessed horses, loaned us some. We finished landing the 12-pounders at College Landing today. The American troops are all disembarked.

The Comte de Rochambeau's army occupied the camp on the left in front of the city tonight behind that of the grenadiers and light infantry. The Comte de Rochambeau talks about this operation, of the way it was put together, his and General Washington's plans for the siege of York and of the ["reconnoitre"? crossed out] most brilliant and satisfying manner.

They did not want to go forward until all the troops and all the 12-pounders and the field artillery were disembarked. Their plan is to first ensure the resources of all kinds that both armies may need and then to invest the place all at once. The army has to march very incessantly on Yorktown. Mr. de Béville asked me to collect all possible information about the country and to draw up detailed itineraries according to reports from the locals. A few people in York gave me materials. I spent the day comparing them and I drew up the attached itineraries according to which the order of march will be decided.

---

235 Claude Gabriel Marquis de Choisy (1723-1800) commanded Lauzun's Legion and General George Weedon's Virginia militia at the siege of Yorktown. They blocked Tarleton's Legion's escape route at Gloucester Point. Choisy was awarded the Libertas Americana medal for his service and retired from active duty in 1793.

The 27th in Williamsburg

A resident of York gave me such clear notes on the position of this city, the land that surrounds it and the enemy works both on the river and toward the land that I have tried to draw up a conjectural plan according to the questions I asked him, although we can't achieve a satisfactory degree of precision. However, a few Williamsburg people examined York's location and found the details of the surroundings truthful. I presented this plan to the Comte de Rochambeau. He reviewed it and compared it with that which engineers had here from some surveyors of the region and which contained no details of the position. I found myself in agreement with this plan for all road junctions. Thus, it is certain that by questioning carefully, by comparing the different responses we can make a quite accurate sketch that is then easily rectified.

["28th" crossed out]

The army's order of march was issued tonight. The Americans will form the vanguard up to a distance of 3 miles from the city where they will go [by] the road on the right. The individual order of march for each army is relative to the rank and place of brigades in the line.

We received news of the arrival of Admiral Digby[236] in New York with 10 or 12 ships. He is on board the *Prince William*. It is said that the first movement of the Comte de Grasse when he heard this news was to put to sea. We don't want him to leave the Chesapeake Bay so as not to risk anything in this important expedition. The

---

236 Admiral Robert Digby (1732–1815) was a Royal Navy officer who also served briefly as a Member of Parliament. He was appointed Admiral of the Red in 1781 and given the command of the North American Station. Digby helped to organize the evacuation of some 1,500 Loyalists to the small port of Conway in Nova Scotia in 1783. The settlement he led transformed the tiny village into a town, which was renamed Digby. The town's museum was also named the Admiral Digby Museum in his honor.

Marquis de Lafayette went aboard *La Ville de Paris* himself to bring the generals' dispatches.

Mr. de Choisy also went to precede Mr. de Grasse to take command of the garrisons of the vessels with which he will go to Gloucester and invest it in concert with the Duc de Lauzun. This one is already there with his legion and 1500 militiamen in the process of joining Mr. de Choisy's corps.

The Touraine, Gatinois and Agénois, Regiments are in good condition, well-seasoned and well organized. The Count d'Autichamp[237] commands the Régiment Agenois. I was very pleased to see him. I reminded him of his kindness to my brother.

We are leaving the baggage depot, the treasury, subsistence of all kinds and hospitals at Williamsburg.

The 28 at Camp in front of York

The army set out to march at dawn according to the prescribed order with each regiment having its field artillery and 12-pounders and howitzers in the front. The Baron de Vioménil commanded the vanguard composed of all the grenadiers and light artillerymen of the army, of Saint-Simon's corps of volunteers and 100 hussars of Lauzun's Legion.

The Comte de Vioménil was at the head of the troops. Count Rochambeau and his entire general staff [2 words crossed out] was between the vanguard and the army. The plan is to invest the city of York today.

And the Americans must have the right of the lines of circumvallation, they marched ahead of us and by the same route up to 3 miles from the city where they took a road on the right that falls back into that of Warwick in order to envelop and restrict the enemy position as much as possible – a mile below the point of separation. The

---

237 Antoine-Joseph-Eulalie de Beaumont, marquis d'Autichamp (1744-1822) commanded the Régiment Agenois. He was promoted to major general in 1782.

Baron of Vioménil detached from his person[238] with the hussars and volunteers, and went to reconnoiter the fort on the enemy's right. As it is defended by the course and the deep ravine of Wind Mill Creek[239] which is very close to the city, they had no advanced guards below the ravine and the city.

The Comte de Rochambeau had the column halt one mile from the edge of the woods where he personally went to observe the enemies. He determined the location of the Agenois regiment's camp and the very place where he had halted the troops blocking the York Road 1/2 mile below the fork (see the map and the itineraries[240]) of the middle of the woods, the left at the beginning of a ravine. This regiment was ordered to clear the left all the way to the river and to push some posts forward to the edge of the woods. After thus supporting his left, the Comte de Rochambeau had the Bourbonnais and Soissonnais regiments march to the right through the woods.

We examined a communication trench from the left to the height of Secretary Nelson's Quarters[241] 2 miles away ["large"? crossed out] by which one could lead the artillery. The Comte de Rochambeau put himself at the head of the column. He [one word crossed out] halted the Soissonnais regiment 1 mile in this direction in a clearing behind Powell's Plantation[242], still pushing forward posts in the woods and cutting all the ["directions"? crossed out] parallel communications at the place and at the distance of 1½ miles. Half a mile away, further in the same direction, we fell into a great road on which the Americans ["by which"? crossed out] had already pushed a few small patrols of dragoons. Here, we were only ½ mile from the

---

238 This expression is translated literally. It means that the Baron de Vioménil left his normal duties/occupations to go with the hussars and volunteers.
239 Wind Mill Point was between Ballard's Creek and Yorktown Creek near where the Fusilier's Redoubt was located on the far right of the British position. 37.24034394780197, -76.5214538128533
240 The map and the itineraries have been separated from the manuscript.
241 37.182423332034254, -76.52222781702727
242 Powell's Plantation was in the area near the Williamsburg Visitor Center. 37.27927562814141, -76.6983652263302

station of Pigeon Hill[243], and not 1/4 of a mile from ["the front of" crossed out] the great guard of the enemies.

The Comte de Rochambeau detached the battalions of grenadiers and light infantry from the Bourbonnais regiment on the left and assigned their camp on the hill in the woods, cutting the paths that lead to Pigeon Hill. He then arrived with the regiment and the 12-pounders attached to it on the hill called Secretary Nelson's Quarters. Here we found General Washington. All his troops had already arrived behind this hill and continued to file by their right. The enemies occupying the camp between the city and the redoubts [three words crossed out] on the edge of the woods, forced the allied army to surround very extensively. Tarleton's Legion which engaged in battle in the field beyond the creek increased the difficulties even more. They were forced to fire 4-pounders. They withdrew. We occupied the main outlets on the field in front of camp and the American army bivouacked behind the right of the French army.

---

243 Pigeon Hill is also known as Penny Hill, or Pigeon Quarter. It was near the junction of Goosely Road and Hampton Road. 37.22518619824562, -76.51863827523151

Fig. 12. French howitzer (left) and a 13-inch mortar at Yorktown. A mortar fires a shell or bomb which is a hollow iron ball filled with gunpowder. It has a large touch-hole for a slow-burning fuse which is held in place by pieces of wood and fastened with a cement made of quicklime, ashes, brick dust, and steel filings worked together with glutinous water. It is fired in a high arc over fortifications and often detonates in the air, raining metal fragments with high velocity on the fort's occupants. Mortars were not mounted on wheeled carriages. Translator's photo.

The generals and general staff of both armies lodged, camped and barracked in the place called Log's field[244] and they will stay there for the duration of the siege. The hospitals and all parts of the administration were left at Williamsburg.

The 29 same

---

244 Unidentified location

The enemies having withdrawn behind their redoubts and the American posts having tightly restricted the forward pickets of the British army, General Washington's troops crossed the swamp, rebuilt the bridge which the enemies had destroyed and continued their movement by their right. The first regiments camped in the field where Tarleton's Legion was, the others, the light infantry under the command of the Marquis de Lafayette successively to the woods in which the riflemen and militiamen were camped. A chain of posts was formed up to the river. The land being extremely open on the left of the enemy and there being a detached structure on the river there which enfilades the entire shoreline, this part could not be surrounded in a strong enough manner nor as close as the others. But all communications are cut off; and, as of today, the place is perfectly invested. We made inspections that have been honored by cannon shots from the place.

The unfortunate and brave Colonel Scammel[245], who was covering a reconnaissance with a party of dragoons, thought he saw two of his men in front of him very close to the enemy works. He ran there and found himself in the hands of the British dragoons. Two of them grabbed the bridle of his horse. He was obliged to surrender his sword. A third fell on him and cowardly fired a carbine shot wounding him mortally.

---

245 Dumas writes Scambell. Colonel Alexander Scammell (1747–1781) was the highest ranking American officer killed during the siege of Yorktown.

Fig. 13. Communication trenches were dug in a zig-zag fashion to prevent an enemy from enfilading an entire trench. Enemy gunfire would only be effective for a short distance. Trenches would have been dug deeper than this to cover the personnel within them. This trench is one at Yorktown, VA. Translator's photo.

It is very difficult to distinguish the form of the works, the salients merge so much to the eye that one can hardly fix on any point until we are closer. My conjectural plan is not bad for the various outlets and I realized that I had failed to raise several questions that would have brought me much closer to the truth.

We received the news of a victory won by General Greene on the British troops 50 miles from Charlestown, after a stubborn and bloody battle. Colonel Washington[246] was wounded and shortly after losing most of his dragoons and having had all his officers killed or wounded. It is to his obstinacy in combat and to the three

---

246 Lieutenant Colonel William Washington (1752–1810) at the battle of Eutaw Springs on Saturday, September 8, 1781.

consecutive charges he made that General Greene had the success of this day. The British are said to have lost 700 men.

The 30

The Bourbonnais Regiment which was camped on the height of Nelson's Quarters went to take the position first occupied by the grenadiers and light infantry of this regiment forward in the woods; and these were brought more forward.

An outpost to the right of the enemy was forced to retreat below Windmill Creek.[247] There were a few musket shots fired. We lost a few men and an officer.

The Americans finished the investment, posted their guards and tightened the place as much as possible.

The enemies evacuated the redoubts of Pigeon's Quarter[248] and Poplar Tree on the Hampton Road. Misters de Bazley and Mauduit,[249] who went to inspect, first entered and came to report to Mr. de Rochambeau. These two redoubts very strong, palisaded, surrounded by abatis covered the British camp. Their outposts were on all roads within musket range of the redoubts. They had blocked the roads with trees and perfectly opened the land from the edge of the woods to the redoubts and from the redoubts to the city. No doubt General Cornwallis feared that the troops employed in guarding these redoubts were not cut off because of their too great a distance from the place and that he preferred to close themselves immediately in a tighter circle rather than risk holding this external position. It seems to me that only the imperfection of the works of

---

247 Windmill Creek is now called Yorktown Creek. 37.23959083333149, -76.51289405546511. During the Revolutionary War, the windmill was on the east side of the creek, near the mouth. Civil War era maps show the windmill on the west side of the creek. Before or during the Civil War, the mill was moved or a new one constructed.
248 Pigeon's Quarter was a British strong redoubt between two ravines. This redoubt was the key to the British position. 37.22559626048289, -76.51752247634637. Poplar Tree was the other strong redoubt. The Poplar Tree Redoubt was where Colonel Scammell was killed. 37.22559626048289, -76.51752247634637
249 Thomas-Antoine de Mauduit du Plessis

the place and the fear of being taken with drawn swords were the only factors that compelled him to make this decision.

If our first attack were successful, it would make our first approaches very easy and they could have contested this position for a long time. We took possession of these redoubts. We stayed there and we immediately planned two intermediaries. I was in the one on the right which is on the way to Hampton and closest to the works. The enemy never ceases firing on the workers but with little effect.

October

On 1ˢᵗ 8ᵇʳᵉ [October] same

I was ordered to go reconnoiter a convenient landing place for the siege artillery and ammunition. It seemed to me that Trebell's Landing[250] was the most suitable being 7 miles from York, quite a nice road, (see the reconnaissance of a point on the James River[251]). I came back to report to the generals and it was decided that the artillery would land at that point.

The engineers took a few points and plotted the land between the outer works and the city. We plan the attacks. Meanwhile, we work to make saucissons[252], gabions[253], fascines[254]. We improve communications between the different camps and especially between the two armies.

Mr. de Choisy, who had left Williamsburg to take command of the garrisons of the ships that must be unloaded on the Gloucester side, has not yet gone. I was ordered to send him the empty convoy ships. Mr. de Villebrune made them leave immediately. There is

---

250 Dumas calls it Tribull's or Treebull's Landing. 37.19762484916337,-76.6230025778812 The artillery and stores of the American and French armies were landed in September 1781. They were then conveyed overland some six miles to the siege lines at Yorktown.
251 This document no longer accompanies the manuscript.
252 Saucissons are long fascines (see note 185) from 18 to 21 feet and 10 or 12 inches in diameter.
253 Gabions are cylindrical baskets made of wicker and filled with earth for use in building fortifications.
254 Fascines are long bundles of sticks tied together, used in building earthworks and in strengthening ramparts.

such agreement between all parties in this operation that the purpose towards which they tend must be achieved. The Duc de Lauzun is on the Gloucester side since the arrival of his legion. A corps of 1500 militiamen joined him there. He is in a position [blank space] distant from the enemy entrenchments.

Fig. 14. Gabions and fascines were used to build and strengthen earthworks. Gabions, the wicker baskets in the rear, were filled with earth and formed the basic structure of the earthwork. The fascines, bundles of branches in the foreground, added to the structure to support the earthworks and to act as a buffer or shock absorber against enemy gunfire.

The 2 8^{ber} [October] same

We hasten the landing of the American and French siege artillery. I went back to Trebell's Landing and I selected a convenient landing site for the Americans on the same beach a little lower than yesterday. I soften the slope of the cliff, and, beginning tomorrow, the ships loaded with artillery will go up the river and come to anchor opposite Trebell's Landing.

Nothing new at the camp. The enemy fires a lot on the redoubts and the curious. I was among that number. I made a little reconnaissance for me alone. I think the land in front of the enemy left is the only one suitable to push attacks. I do not understand that Lord Cornwallis did not defend his first position whose right is all cut with ravines, and the entire left protected by his damaged outworks and by ravines less [illegible] deep than those on his right. The enemy right is [illegible] very strong by the nature of the land and cannot be approached because of the steepness of the escarpments.

The 3rd same

Same work, the redoubts have been perfected. We resolve the plan of attack. The enemy fires lively during the night, especially to keep away the workers who could open the trench. We unload the artillery with the greatest activity. I repaired the roads that had been degraded in the crossing of the creeks. We took two observation points on the York River above and below the city. From here, we can see perfectly the anchorage of the enemy ships and the opposite shore on the Gloucester side. The *Charon*, the frigate and the transport ships are anchored across the river in the channel between Gloucester and the chain of broken and sunken ships. A small brig and the frigate go up the river up to ½ mile above this position and cannonade all that appears on the shore. Mr. de Choisy landed with 800 men, drawn from the garrisons of the ships. He joined the Duc de Lauzun, and he approaches Gloucester to take a position between the two creeks one mile from the enemy works and thus closing their back door.

We saw all of Tarleton's legion cross the river. All the negroes were put out of the place. Most are dying or infected with contagious diseases. [one word crossed out]

The 4th same

We ask for artillery. We are impatient. We would like that the trench were opened, but our generals who have a good game and who do not want to spoil it will not allow us to open the trench only when we have parts to put in battery and that they will be sufficiently supplied. We heard very strong musketry fire this morning and we noticed a lot of troop movements at Gloucester. I am still very busy with landing the artillery.

The 5th same

The general received letters from Mr. Choisy who informs him that having carried forward his position to go take the one between the two creeks, Lord Cornwallis had Colonel Tarleton make a sortie[255]. Mr. de Choisy repulsed the British troops after a very sharp fire on Mr. Tarleton's cavalry. The Duc de Lauzun charged Colonel Tarleton's cavalry himself at the head of his company of lancers. The colonel himself was dragged by the fugitives. He fell from his horse and all his troop passed over him. The Duc de Lauzun took his horse—

The engineers have finished planning the attacks. We had to open the trench today. The enemy is harassed every night by patrols that will fire shots to the structures in order to divide their forces and attention.

The 6 - same

---

255 A sortie is an attack made by the besieged to destroy the besieger's works, stop his progress, spike his guns, etc.

Appendix 1

The following "Reconnaissance of the positions at Portsmouth and of the British works in this part of Virginia" appears as an appendix in the Comte de Lauberdière's journal (http://gallica.bnf.fr/ark:/12148/btv1b52506900t/f17.image cahier 3 folios 155-160). The penmanship is finer than that of the rest of Lauberdière's journal, so he probably did not copy it. The document also appears pretty much verbatim in the first part of the Christian Deux Ponts papers (Pfalzische Landesbibliothek 18) and seems to be in the same hand as the one in Lauberdière's journal but the layout of the pages is different and some numbers spelled out in one document are written in numerals in the other. At the top of the page of the copy in the Deux Ponts papers is a note "Duplicata du No. 9." At the end of the report, another note reads: "at Portsmouth, November 1, 1781, signed Dumas assistant quartermaster general." However, the scribe's penmanship is very different from that in Dumas's journal and from the rest of the documents in the Deux Ponts papers.

Reconnaissance of the positions at Portsmouth and of the British works in this part of Virginia.

I divide the reconnaissance of this position in exterior and interior. To wit:
----

1. The region of Portsmouth extends 10 or 12 miles and includes the different branches of the Elizabeth River and the mouths near Cape Henry and toward North Carolina.

2. The position of Portsmouth itself and the details of the British works

Article 1 Exterior Reconnaissance

The Elizabeth River which empties into the James River opposite Hampton Bay is wide and about 4 miles from its mouth. Its course runs to Norfolk. Portsmouth is only 8 or 9 miles away. It is divided into three branches called Eastern Branch, Southern Branch and Western Branch according to the points on the compass.

The Western Branch which we leave on the right going up river takes its source about 16 miles inland at a location called Hall.

The source of the South Branch is in the marsh at Great Bridge, 19 miles above Portsmouth by water and 10 miles by land. It is divided in two branches by a spit of land called Ferry Point. The cities or rather Portsmouth and Norfolk are on opposite sides of the river, Portsmouth on the left bank, Norfolk on the right.

The East Branch has its source a little above Kemp's Landing 12 miles from Norfolk by water and 8 miles by land.

Other than these main branches there are also various creeks, in the Elizabeth River and in the three branches which form it, which go more or less inland, making their banks very muddy.

The Elizabeth River is navigable as far as Lambert Crossing[256] and to Pinner's Point[257] for all vessels which are able to enter the James River. We find a bar above Pinner's Point which only vessels of 90 guns or less can cross. The frigates and the transport vessels cannot go upriver any higher than Ferry Point.

From the point to the outskirts of Portsmouth, nature is the same everywhere. The terrain is very flat. There are very large marshes and pine groves interspersed among the plantations.

---

256 Lambert's Point
257 Pinner Point is a cape in Portsmouth opposite Lambert's Point. I is situated north of Sugar Hill, close to Bruce Johnson Memorial Park.

The main passages across the marsh which separates this state from North Carolina are at the head of the three branches of the Elizabeth River. And it is there that the location of Portsmouth is so very important. These three points are called Kemp's Landing on the East Branch, Great Bridge on the South Branch and Hall on the Western branch.

To go from Cape Henry to Norfolk, one must go by
Kemp's Landing   12 miles
from Kemp's Landing to Norfolk   8
              total   20 miles

to go from Cape Henry to Ferry Point, opposite Portsmouth
one has to go by Kemp's Landing   12 miles
 from Kemp's Landing to Ferry Point   7
              total   19 miles

To go from Cape Henry to North Carolina one has to pass by
Kemp's Landing   12 miles
Kemp's Landing to Great Bridge   8 miles
Great Bridge to Great Swamp, Carolina   18
              total   38 m

There is a direct route from Ferry Point to Great Bridge 10 miles distant.

Along this route, 3 miles from Ferry Point, we find the beginning of a road which goes to Kemp's Landing and which is called Princess Anne Road, 4 miles from Kemp's Landing and 7 miles from Great Bridge.

Great Bridge was fortified. The bridge was cut and a good star fort erected on the right of the road on a small island formed by the marsh. This fort was surrounded by a moat, a double abatis and four rows of trails in checkerboard pattern. It was at the center of the three roads, that of Ferry Point, that of Carolina, and that of Suffolk.

In the corner of the space between Great Bridge and the ocean is an impassable marsh. To avoid this location and to enter Carolina, one has to land at Carituk[258] just 3 miles south of Cape Henry.

The post of Hall on the Suffolk road where [unintelligible] the British posted a small body of light troops. They constructed two strong redoubts in front of their camps and beside the brook. That on the left is on the road by the right because of the muddy course of the Western Branch nor from the left because of the large marsh which extends from there to Great Bridge. The communication between these two posts is through the large marsh. There is only this single dike. The marsh is still on the right and several creeks on the left which empty into the South Branch.

To go from Portsmouth to Suffolk, one has to pass through Hall
   12 M.
Subtotal 12

Hall to Suffolk on the Nansemond River
   14
Total 26 M

to go from Hall to Great Bridge one has to pass by the great dike
   4
from the dike to Carberey's Mill
   3
from Carberey's Mill to Great Bridge
   7
———
Total 14 Miles

I will not speak here of any other detail of the terrain around Portsmouth. I tried to express them on the map. I also marked the posts which the large British guards occupied in the various directions.

---

258 Currituck

Article 2 Interior Reconnaissance

The British remained masters of the sea while they occupied Portsmouth. Having to fear only parties from Norfolk or Ferry Point, they had not sought to defend the anchorage off Portsmouth. Their vessels were anchored when they were on the defensive, preventing vessels of lesser force from going upriver. They also had not constructed batteries on their most vulnerable sides. They only erected the old fort at this point at the last minute. This fort, formerly built by the Americans, was very large. I think, by its size, it could hold 90 pieces of cannon of different caliber in the battery. The British under the command of Colonel Matthews[259] landed in the Western branch in the month of May 1779. They captured, by land, the fort which was weekly defended. They demolished the batteries, spiked the cannons and scratched on a post Mind the back doors[260]. There are still several pieces of cannon in this fort with damaged trunnions.

We also see the remains of an American battery at the tip of Portsmouth.

Portsmouth is built on a flat and open bank between two creeks which form a peninsula of about 400 square toises [780 square yards] located between the ends of their closest branches at a distance of 190 toises [405 yards]. There are not 10 to 16 to the bend. A slow rising hill and the course of the creeks was just the advantage we could draw from the land. The creek on the left is impassable everywhere. It suffices to raise a few small works to close the position and to prevent their small boats to go upriver in different branches. There was once a dike on this creek which the British destroyed and on which they had directed some embrasures of a large work which was at the head of this Creek.

The creek on the right was not as wide and did not go up as high as the other. The enemy fortified the interior slope by a series(?) of detached works. They constructed a dam to retain the tidal water

---

259 Lieutenant Colonel Edward Mathew (1729–1805)
260 repeated in French

and made the flow the foundation to the head of the creek. They took advantage of the mill on the other side of the creek to defend the head of the dike. This mill was crenellated and covered with a curtain, surrounded by a double abatis. They placed three fieldpieces on the platform which dominated all the exterior. The works which were in the center of the position between the two large redoubts which covered the head of the two creeks were all open from the gorge and all these gaps were defended by a large abatis.

I will not go into any greater detail. I prepared the map with the greatest precision possible. And the measurement of the development of the fortifications on the right and left could serve as a guide. I will only note that all the works which I had razed were solidly constructed, covered with fascines inside and out. The parapets were 15 to 18 feet thick on the land side. The line of fire seemed very extended to me and to consider this position from the land side, it would be considered strong.

Measurements of the British Works at Portsmouth

Blockhouses at the mouth of the creek on the right and redan in front of the moat with an embrasure   19 toises
Dams, dikes and sewers formed around three embrasures, behind the dike, fortified mill at the head of the dike   122 toises
Curtains flanked by two half bastions[261]   47 toises
Closed redoubt of 3 embrasures along the creek   60 toises

Two redoubts on the shore of the creek behind the above work
    29 toises
Large closed redoubt with 7 embrasures flanking the works at the head of the creek   96 toises
Battery of 3 embrasures defending the area around the ford at the head of the creek   11 toises

---

261 A bastion is a fortification with a projecting part of a wall to protect the main walls of the fortification.

Large redoubt of 6 embrasures, main work between the two creeks
72 toises

Suite of covered works by the gorge between the above redoubt and that which is at the head of the creek on the left

To wit

Barbette battery in the center	86 toises
On the attack front	86 toises
two redoubts	86 toises
the mill converted to a bombproof powder magazine on the left of the bomb	86 toises
large closed redoubt of 6 embrasures at the head of the creek on the left with a covered battery by the gorge 2 or 3 embrasures linked to the works	60 toises

Last works on the left along the creek

To wit

Redan facing the dike	45 toises
other redan	45 toises
closed star redoubt and three embrasures	45 toises
total	643 French toises [1370 yards]

Signed Dumas, assistant quartermaster general

Appendix 2

The handwriting of this document seems to be that of the same scribe who transcribed the "Reconnaissance of the positions at Portsmouth and of the British works in this part of Virginia." That script differs from that in the rest of the Deux Ponts papers where this document was found. It also differs from that of Mathieu Dumas in the draft diary which is the main focus of this volume. However, the content of this document seems to have been written by Dumas. First, it follows the "Reconnaissance of the positions at Portsmouth" which concludes with the note that it was composed by Dumas. The two documents complement each other and were transcribed by the same scribe. Second, they appear together in the Deux Ponts papers so they seem to have been kept as a unit. Third, the writing style resembles that of Dumas and includes lengthy passages of natural history, just as his draft diary wherein Dumas notes "I love trees." Later, he observes "I speak constantly about the trees." This document is very specific about the trees and shrubs he observes. Finally, many of the observations he makes are consistent with the concerns an engineer or a quartermaster would have.

Travels in Virginia in 1782

I left Williamsburg on April 7 with Mr. Mead, a well-regarded man in his town and worthy of being so. I crossed the James River from Jamestown to Cobham[262] and the first city or, better said, the

---
262 Cobham was on the shore of the James River. Opposite Jamestown.

first village I encountered was Smithfield[263], 22 miles from Cobham. It contains about 200 houses and it is the capital of the county called Isle of Wight. Its location is pleasant, being situated between two creeks which give it the form of a peninsula. One of these creeks is large enough to accommodate ships of 200 tons to go upriver. Commerce is conducted primarily in the islands in tobacco, tar and salted meat which are the products of the region. Some people sent ships to Nantes which seems to be the place the Americans chose for commerce. There are others which have outfitted privateers with some success.

After an excellent dinner at Col. Parker's[264], my travel companion brought me to Mr. Cooper[265] 15 miles from there where we had a good supper, good wine and a good bed. I left on the 8th and, after having travelled 7 miles, I arrived at Suffolk. I only saw ruins. Suffolk was burned by the British in 1779, in an expedition commanded by Col. Mathews[266]. A few houses were rebuilt. This little town which ought to be a little larger than Smithfield, is located on the Nansemond Creek which goes to the James River. Ships of 250 tons go upriver. Her trade and that of Nansemond County, of which it is the capitol, consists of tar and turpentine of which it exports 60,000 barrels and 12,000 of salted meat. There is no, or almost no trade in tobacco. I attended the election of the two delegates that the county sends to the general assembly. The voters took care to get inebriated before voting, according to the custom religiously observed in all of America on such occasions and which this free people does not seem at all disposed to renounce.

After dinner, I departed with Mr. Mead and Col. Parker who came to join us. We slept at Dismal Swamp[267], a name which it

---

263 Written Schmitsfield, Smithfield is about 18 miles southeast of Jamestown
264 Josiah Parker (1751–1810)
265 Written Copper
266 Lieutenant Colonel Edward Mathew (1729–1805)
267 The name is given in English and explained in French. The Great Dismal Swamp is a large swamp in the Coastal Plain Region of southeastern Virginia and northeastern North Carolina, between Norfolk, Virginia, and Elizabeth City, North Carolina. It is now a National Wildlife Refuge.

earned by its somber and wild appearance. This swamp was given to a company which was charged with clearing it, but which has yet done almost nothing.

We lodged at the farmer of the company named Collu[268]. He owns the finest farm I have ever seen in America. It is located to the west of the swamp, on a place a little higher than the rest of the area and contains about 400 acres. To get there, one has to cross a mile of this swamp. In his beautiful home, everything speaks of ease, industry and this sweet and peaceful happiness, so rarely disturbed because it is not envied and the people who enjoy it are content.

The farmer is a man of about 60 years old, of untiring energy which he communicates to the entire family. He is married and has seven children. Four are of working age and who, together with their mother, make all the cloth necessary to clothe the family and 18 Blacks will belong to the farm. The farmer grows flax and cotton needed to make these fabrics. His flocks which feed only off the pastures of the swamp furnish the fabrics. The indigo, which he grows successfully, serves to dye the fabrics. His wife and children card the wool and the cotton, prepare the linen, spin and work at the task. Thus, their labors give them linen cloth, cotton cloth and a mixed fabric of wool and cotton warm enough for the winter.

This farm which is about 400 acres is the only clearing that the company accomplished. It brings in 3500 bushels of corn per year. A bushel produces 60 pounds of flour which makes 210,000 pounds. We made a test with rice: 4 acres produced 12,000 pounds which sells in town for 72[269] pence a pound. The 4 acres alone produce £3600. The test of indigo was very successful. Judging by what was done, the clearing of the swamp will be a source of immense riches.

The 9th, we saw the lake which is about in the middle of the swamp, from west to east. We traveled in a pirogue[270] on a canal 8 miles long and about eight or 10 feet wide. Its maintenance is

---

268 The name is written Colln or Collu.
269 The number is left blank in the manuscript.
270 Pirogue is a flat-bottomed boat six to 20 feet long with flaring sides and a sharp bow used for fishing and transportation in the swamps and bayous. Propelled by paddles or poles.

neglected and we arrived at the lake not without difficulty. Not only were we on the verge of hauling several times, but we were constantly obliged to fight against tree branches and the thorns which blocked our route. Finally, I arrived at the lake where I enjoyed the most extraordinary view which I ever saw. It presents a sheet of water from 20 to 24 miles in circumference. It is 5 or 6 miles from north to south and 4 from East to West. Its greatest depth is 14 feet. Its shores are covered with enormous trees. The most notable is the cypress whose branches, bending sadly to the ground, recall to our soul the eternal rest which we will someday find there. We see very large tree trunks floating in the lake and, at the same time, some trunks whose roots still cling to the earth. Their extremities seem to have been burned which leads us to surmise that this lake was once a swamp like the rest of Dismal Swamp which the thunder or another cause entirely might have ignited a fire and that it was a fire which produced this immense excavation. Without putting any faith in this assumption, the fact is not impossible. An experiment the farmer made in a time of drought proved that this marshland, the deadwood which is buried there or which covers it and the reeds which are in great quantity are so much combustible material capable of producing a fire.

In crossing the farm to the lake, I found black earth of an excellent quality everywhere.

The known fish of the lake are the perch, the eel, the gudgeon, the catfish, the blackfish, the turtle and the terrapin which is a type of turtle, but which cannot enclose itself in its shell like the turtle and whose tail is covered with little pointed scales.

To the west of the swamp, entering it, we find the following types of trees: the white oak, the poplar or tulip tree, the gumtree, the beech, the common pine, the ash, the holly or holly oak[271]. Upon advancing toward the lake we find-- the cypress again, the red or white cedar, the maple, the laurel, the reeds which are of a type more compact and thicker than ours and which very much

---

271 each tree has a corresponding French name.

resemble cane, without being so perfect, the elm, the juniper which much resembles pine and is an excellent wood for construction. In the less marshy areas, we find the [unintelligible] and the dogwood whose flowers are very pretty.

Among the bushes we find the boxwood which is a type of laurel, the magnolia or little Laurel, the yellow jasmine, black and green thorn, rattan, the breakly ash. The wood of the latter resembles the elder, straight as a cane. Its greatest height is 8 or 9 feet. It grows from sprouts. Each sprout is marked by a spiny covering. It is without branches and has a small tuft of foliage at its peak. It is said it is very poisonous. The outer covering is tern and gray, the second green, the third white. The poison resides mainly in the second. To these shrubs, I would add another which the residents have not yet given a name. It has the leaves of a strawberry. The leaves have a fragrance similar to that of the rose when we rub them a little. Rose bushes and raspberry bushes are very common.

The inhabitants of the woods, other than the men whom the thirst for riches and hardship drives everywhere, are the bears and the panther. I say panther, according to the designation of the local inhabitants. I thought they mistook the bear for the panther. I expressed my doubts. They insisted and, according to the description which they gave me about the color of this animal and its size which they say surpasses that of the largest dog, it is probable that it is a true panther, possibly a little smaller than the one from Africa, because all the animals of this new continent seem to be inferior to those of the old. The bear is equally much smaller and more timid than the bears of Europe. They are not even strong enough to attack the cattle and the cows which are left to pasture in the swamps and which are only fearful to the pigs and sheep. Other than these two formidable animals, we find the wildcat, the deer which resemble our buck, except that it is not speckled, the raccoon, the possum, the hare, the otter, and the muskrat.

The reptiles are the rattlesnake which is rather rare, the water moccasin, also very poisonous, the copper belly and the black snake[272]. These last two types are not poisonous. There are also several others whose names are unknown.

I will note here, with regret, that the Americans are in the greatest ignorance regarding the natural history of their country while it would offer a vast field of knowledge to a naturalist. Their unconcern is at such a point that they do not make any effort to know the anti-venomous plants which nature has given them to heal fatal snakebites from the rattlesnake and a few other poisonous animals. The savage uses an herb with which he immediately heals himself. The American almost always dies from the bite or injection which wounded him.

Bad weather detained me at Dismal Swamp the 10th and 11th. I departed on the 12th, not without regretting my hosts. I sadly left the abode of candor, of innocence, filial piety, conjugal love and of every domestic virtue. I wish for the happiness of this respectable family for the even more impenetrable obstacles which the swamps in which it has withdrawn. The joys of the two eldest daughters, their purity, their candor, are an added charm for seduction, less fearful because they are very virtuous. Their arms against corruption are very weak. I arrived at Portsmouth the night of the 12th and I had the time that evening to see the works constructed by Leslie[273] and Arnold.

The creek, from its mouth to the grand redoubt marked No. 6 on the map and which is beside the redoubt by which the Suffolk Road passes is impassable. The rest of this creek is [fordable] and is crossed with the greatest ease. The British attempted to block the passage with a lock which cannot bring more than 3 feet of water. This part actually fordable is about 100 toises [213 yards]. There are 150 toises [320 yards] from one creek to the other in the closest parts. That is the attackable front.

The creek on the left presents many difficulties but they are not insurmountable. It is not so much the creek which is difficult, but the shores which are very muddy. Also, the enemy contented

---

272   each reptile has a corresponding name or description in French.
273   Brigadier General Alexander Leslie (1740-1794) and Benedict Arnold (1741-1801).

himself with constructing very few works to defend this part. He focused all his attention on the center and on the right.

However, it does not appear that he was able to hold out very long. The works were easy to capture from behind from a battery which we would have established on the other side of the creek on the left, in front of a demolished white house. This battery would take from behind the works marked nos 1, 2, 3, 4, 5 on the map from a distance of 250 to 600 toises [532-1278 yards].

If we believed it was necessary to establish a parallel, it could have been done at 250 toises by abutting the right and left on the two creeks. If we want to inconvenience the place even more, the Elizabeth River above Norfolk is not 600 toises and we could have established a battery which, joined with the others, would not have left a single place covered in Portsmouth.

I consider Portsmouth a very poor location, but as Portsmouth is linked to exterior posts which are 10 and 12 miles distant, we have to consider the three points of Kemp's Landing[274], Great Bridge and Hall's as belonging to it.

The three posts I just named are those which defend the region around Portsmouth, particularly Great Bridge and Hall's by which it is necessary to pass to arrive. The guard at these different posts required many men especially Hall's and Kemp's Landing. They can sustain themselves only with 3000 men each. I think 1000 would suffice for Great Bridge. It is true that we could abandon Kemp's Landing where the British kept men only to protect the forages they made in the region.

It therefore required another 4000 men for the defense of the advance posts of Portsmouth, but an army such as Cornwallis's could not make such a large detachment, which was more than half of his force, without exposing the main post upon which we could arrive by a debarkation.

This position could defend itself against the Americans; but it became untenable against the land army and a superior naval force;

---

274 Written as Camp's Landing.

and I am convinced that all the men of war would approve of Lord Cornwallis for having preferred the position of York.

Observations on Porto Cabello

Porto Cabello[275] is located at 40° 12 minutes latitude and belongs to the province of Caracas which was discovered by Ponce de Leon[276] a distinguished family in Spain. Descendants of this Ponce de Leon can still be found in this province.

What is called the city is located in an island which communicates with the mainland by two bridges the largest of which is two toises [4 yards]. It is fortified very irregularly. The ramparts and the parapets are rolling masonry. The batteries which are raised are too formidable to vessels for this place to have nothing to fear and the use of red balls and bombs was not spared. The attack is almost as difficult on the land side.

The two communication bridges of which we just spoke, lead to the suburb which is a mile-long, including a few Negro cabins, and there is another mile from there to the mountains. The heights to the right of the Valencia[277] road (going out of the city) are furnished with three forts which sweep the plain and whose fire crosses with that of the city, which makes any regular approach impossible before capturing these three forts which are very difficult to access.

If the enemy landed in this plane (and he could not descend elsewhere), the suburb, according to the plan of defense, should be burned and the bridges destroyed.

The city goes from north to south. We enter from the south. This part as well as the west where the port is and where the vessels

---

275 Puerto Cabello is on the north coast of Venezuela. It is located in Carabobo State, about 210 km west of Caracas.
276 Juan Ponce de León (1474 –1521) was a Spanish explorer and conquistador known for leading the first official European expedition to Florida and serving as the first governor of Puerto Rico.
277 Valencia is the capital city of Carabobo State and the third-largest city in Venezuela.

can anchor within musket range of the place is defended by the batteries of the city.

The entrance to the port is to the west. It is defended by the crossfire of the city and one fort constructed opposite the city, on the other side of the entrance. The east is surrounded by impassable swamps.

The port is nothing more than a very large cove which can be 12 miles in circumference. It is also surrounded by impassable swamps. The Spanish pretended that as many as 40 ships of the line could enter. I could not yet ascertain the truth of this pretension, but our ships preferred to remain in port, rather than enter this cove, except those which needed repairs are obliged to come into the pass, against the wharf. As soon as they are repaired, they leave.

What is more reasonable to believe about the number of ships that port can contain is that it could effectively contain them if it were put in a state to do so. It would require a lot of mud to be dredged. We pretend that this work would not be difficult.

The province of Caracas still contains at this time (according to what Mr. de Rasa the king's lieutenant in this province told me) more than 200,000 Indians who occupy entire villages in the interior of the region where we can find no whites. They have magistrates of their nation and govern themselves by their own laws with the consent of the Spanish government.

These Indians are not as tall as the savages of North America. Their height is 5 feet 3 to 6 feet. Even though they no longer have a beard, they don't have a more effeminate appearance. However, their bodies are well-built and muscled. Their color is a little redder than that of the Indians in the north.

They are decided enemies of work. Experience has even taught the Spanish that their constitution is too feeble to utilise, even though they might be disposed. Weakness and laziness of the native race lead the Spanish to believe in the cross with the Negroes. The children resulting from these marriages are more energetic, more intelligent and more industrious than the Indians.

Voyage to Carragne[278]

I left Porto Cabello on March 15 with the Comte de Fersen and Misters Dubourg and Schmitt, and we arrived at Valencia the following day. It is only three leagues from the city that we enter the plain which is very narrow at the mouth but widens imperceptibly to the point of being two leagues wide even at Valencia. It is bordered by bald and arid mountains where we can only see aloes. (The itinerary indicates the road and the region, before arriving at the plain.)

Arriving at Valencia, I went to Mr. Marterici, commander of a battalion of troops of Caracas, who speaks French well enough. He brought me to Mr. Pays, the head of justice and captain of grenadiers in the regional militia. Mr. Pays lodged me and gave me and my travel companions dinner and supper. After dinner I was conducted to a hill near the city from where I observed a rather lovely and level region.

Valencia is situated in a plain two leagues wide from north east to the south. Its length stretches beyond the horizon. Beyond that, the plain ends through which the Porto Cabello Road passes as well as the road to Caracas. Valencia has a population of 10,000 men according to Don Marterici. The proportion of whites to Indians is 1 to 10. We counted that there were 6200 men in the province of Caracas, both veterans (this is what they call the white soldiers there) and militia and companies of Negroes. 10,000 men could be mustered. After that, judging by the troops which are at Chile or Peru, Mexico, Paraguay, Santa Fe, at Guatemala, in Florida, California etc. the King of Spain must have, in the New World, an army as numerous as that of Xerxes.

I had the occasion to speak with Mr. Marterici about the Peruvian revolt. The head of the revoluionaries was Tupacamara[279], a true descendent of the ancient house of the Incas whose name is still

---

278 Probably today's Cerro Carangano, about 20 miles west of Caracas.
279 Túpac Amaru (1545 –1572) was the last monarch (Sapa Inca) of the Neo-Inca State, the remnants of the Inca Empire in Vilcabamba, Peru.

revered and cherished by the unfortunate people which groaned for so long a time under Spanish despotism and greed. Unhappiness has not yet erased from their souls the memory of the benefits they enjoyed under the government of their legitimate sovereigns. Ten or 12 years earlier, Tupacamara gave umbrage to the court of Madrid. The governor of Peru was ordered to personally seize him and send him to Madrid; but the Indians took care to conceal him from the political unrest of a monarch they rightfully regarded as a usurper. The Peruvians, believing the time favorable and moreover apparently incited by the British, erupted in 1780.

Sources and Bibliography

Archives

Correspondence of La Luzerne with the Minister of Foreign Affairs, (16 July 1781) Archives Diplomatiques de la Courneuve, 230 PAAP/4.

Dossier Comte Dumas » and « État Militaire Dumas, Archives Nationales LH/843/35.

From George Washington to Dumas, 24 June 1797. founders.archives.gov/documents/Washington/06-01-02-0167.

Letter of De Kalb to Vergennes, (27 sept 1778), Archives Nationales series AAE, CP, Etats Unis 5.

Letter of Montbarrey to Rochambeau, (9 March 1780), Library of Congress, Rochambeau Papers, II, folio 68 (microfilm).

Rochambeau to Montbarrey, on board the Duc de Bourgogne (5 May 1780), Archives Militaires, A1 3733, fol 49.

To George Washington from Gabriel-Mathieu, Comte Dumas, 24 January 1797.
founders.archives.gov/documents/Washington/99-01-02-00214

To Alexander Hamilton from Marquis de Lafayette, 8 December 1797.
founders.archives.gov/documents/Hamilton/01-21-02-0180.

To Alexander Hamilton from Mathieu Dumas, 8 December 1797.
founders.archives.gov/documents/Hamilton/01-21-02-0179.

Bibliography

Aldridge, Alfred Owen. *Benjamin Franklin et Ses Contemporains Français*. M. Didier, 1963.

Anderson, Fred. *Crucible of War: The Seven Years' War and the Fate of Empire in British North America, 1754-1766*. 1st ed., Alfred A. Knopf, 2000.

Bailyn, Bernard. *The Ideological Origins of the American Revolution*. Belknap Press of Harvard University Press, 1967.

Balch, T., *Les Français en Amérique Pendant la Guerre d'Indépendance Américaine 1777-1783*. (Paris 1872).

Blaufarb, Rafe. *The French Army, 1750-1820: Careers, Talent, Merit*. Manchester University Press, 2017.

Bodinier, Gilbert. *Dictionnaire des Officiers Généraux de l'Armée Royale, 1763-1792*. Archives & Culture, 2009.

Bodinier, Gilbert. *Les Officiers de l'Armée Royale: Combattants de la Guerre d'Indépendance des Etats-Unis, de Yorktown À* .... Service Historique De L'Armée De Terre, 1983.

Bourgerie, Raymond, and Pierre Lesouef. *Yorktown (1781): La France Offre l'Indépendance À L›Amérique*. Economica, 1992.

Bourgerie, Raymond, and Pierre Lesouef. *Yorktown (1781): La France Offre l'Indépendance à l'Amérique*. Economica, 1992.

Brandon, Edgar Ewing, editor. *A Pilgrimage of Liberty: A Contemporary Account of the Triumphal Tour of General Lafayette through the Southern and Western States in 1825, as Reported by the Local Newspapers*. Lawhead Press, 1944.

Broadwater, Robert P. *American Generals of the Revolutionary War: A Biographical Dictionary*. Mcfarland, 2012.

Broglin, E., « La révolution américaine », in Poussou, Jean-Pierre. *Le Bouleversement de l'Ordre du Monde: Révoltes et Révolutions en Europe et Aux Amériques à la Fin du XVIIIe Siècle*. Sedes, 2005.

Burn, Robert. *A Naval and Military Technical Dictionary of the French Language: In Two Parts: French-English and English-French; with Explanations of the Various Terms*. 5th ed., J. Murray, 1870.

Caron François. *La Guerre Incomprise, Ou, la Victoire Volée: Bataille de la Chesapeake, 1781*. Service Historique De La Marine, 1989.

Caron, Jean-Claude. *La France de 1815 À 1848*. Troisième édition. Armand Colin, 2013.

Carson, George Barr. *The Chevalier de Chastellux, Soldier and Philosopher*. University of Chicago, 1942.

Cenat, J.P. « Les fonctions de maréchal général des logis à l'époque de Louis XVI », *Revue Historique des Armées*, n. 257, 2009. https://journals.openedition.org/rha/6874

Chaline, Olivier, et al. *La France et l'Indépendance Américaine*. PUPS, Presses de l'Université Paris-Sorbonne, 2008.

Chaline, Olivier. La Mer et la France: Quand les Bourbons Voulaient Dominer les Océans. Paris: Flammarion, 2018.

Chastellux François Jean de. *Voyages De M. Le Marquis De Chastellux Dans l'Amérique Septentrionale*. Prault, 1786. Reprint *Voyages Dans l'Amérique Septentrionale Dans les Années 1780, 1781 Et 1782*. 1ère réédition depuis 1788, augm. d'une notice bibliographique, d'annexes et de lettres inédites en français, de Washington à Chastellux. J. Tallandier, 1980.

    Travels in North-America in the Years 1780, 1781, and 1782. New York Times, *1968.*

Chinard, Gilbert. *Alexandre Berthier; Journal De La Campagne D'amérique, 10 Mai 1780-26 Août 1781. Publié d'après le Manuscrit Inédit de L'université de Princeton*. Institut Français de Washington, 1951.

Closen, Ludwig, et al. *The Revolutionary Journal of Baron Ludwig Von Closen, 1780-1783*. Published for the Institute of Early American History and Culture at Williamsburg, Va. by the University of North Carolina Press, 1958.

Colleville, Ludovic. *Les Missions Secrètes de Général-Major Baron De Kalb: et Son Rôle Dans la Guerre de l'Indépendance Américaine.* 1885.

Contenson, Ludovic de. *La Société Des Cincinnati de France et la Guerre d'Amérique: 1778-1783*. Facsim. reprint. Originally published: Paris: A. Picard, 1934 ed., A. Picard, 2007. https://www.cincinnatidefrance.fr/.

Cottret, Bernard. *La Révolution Américaine: La Quête Du Bonheur, 1763-1787*. [Nouv. éd.] ed., Perrin, 2012.

Couzigou, Jean-Vincent. *L'Aigle et le Lys: l'Épopée des Combattants Français des Deux Guerres de l'Indépendance Américaine.* Muller édition, 2007.

Cromot Du Bourg, Marie Francois Joseph Maxime, Comte de. Diary of a French Officer, 1781. *The Magazine of American history with notes and queries.* New York: A.S. Barnes, 1877, 1893 4 (1880) pp. 205-214, 293-308, 376-385, 441-452; 7 (1881) 283-295.

D'Orleans, J. et de Trentinian, J., « La victoire de la Chesapeake et de Yorktown, 5 septembre-19 octobre 1781 », http://www.cincinnatidefrance.fr/histoire/172-la-victoire-de-la-chesapeake-et-d-yorktown-5-septembre-19-octobre-1781.

de Trentinian, Jacques. *La France Au Secours de l'Amerique.* SPM, 2016.

Doniol Henri. *Histoire de la Participation de la France à l'Établissement des Etats-Unis d'Amerique : Correspondance Diplomatique et Documents.* Imprimerie Nationale/France, 1886.

Dumas, Mathieu, and Ambroise Tardieu. *Précis des Évènemens Militaires, Ou Essais Historiques sur les Campagnes de 1799 à 1814: Avec Cartes et Plans.* Chez Treuttel Et Würtz, 1816.

Dumas, Mathieu. *Souvenirs Du Lieutenant-Général Cte Mathieu Dumas, de 1770 À 1836.* C. Gosselin, 1839. Excerpts were translated into English as *Memoirs of his Own Time; Including the Revolution, the Empire, and the Restoration.* By Lieut.-Gen. Count Mathieu Dumas. London: Richard Bentley, 1839.

The period covered by this diary can be found on pp. 37-91 of vol. 1 of the *Souvenirs* and pp. 53-65 of vol. 1 of the *Memoirs*.

Durand, John. *New Materials for the History of the American Revolution.* H. Holt, 1889.

Dziembowski, Edmond. *La Guerre De Sept Ans: 1756-1763*. Perrin, 2018.

Ferling, John E. *Almost a Miracle: The American Victory in the War of Independence*. Book Club ed., Oxford University Press, 2007.

Ferling, John E. *Independence: The Struggle to Set America Free*. 1st U.S. ed., 1st U.S. ed., Bloomsbury Press, 2011.

Ferreiro, Larrie D. *Brothers at Arms: American Independence and the Men of France & Spain Who Saved It*. Vintage Books, 2017.

Fersen, Hans Axel von, and Fredrik Axel von Fersen. *Lettres d'Axel de Fersen À Son Père: Pendant La Guerre de l'Indépendance d'Amérique*. Edited by F. U Wrangel, Firmin-Didot Et Cie, 1929.

Girault de Coursac, Paul, and Pierrette Girault de Coursac. *Guerre d'Amérique et Liberté des Mers*. O.E.I.L, 1993.

Greene, Jerome A. *The Guns of Independence: The Siege of Yorktown, 1781*. 1st ed., 1st ed., Savas Beatie, 2005.

Hallahan, William H. *The Day the Revolution Ended, 19 October 1781*. Castle Books, 2006.

Heitman Francis Bernard. *Historical Register of the Officers of the Continental Army during the War of the Revolution: April, 1775, to December, 1783*. Rare Book Shop Pub. Co., 1914. http://www.carolana.com/SC/Revolution/Historical_Register_of_the_Officers_of_the_Continental_Army_Francis_B_Heitman_1914.pdf

Hoffman, Ronald, et al. *Diplomacy and Revolution: The Franco-American Alliance of 1778*. Published for the United States Capitol Historical Society by the University Press of Virginia, 1981.

Kaspi André. *L'Indépendance Américaine: 1763-1789*. Gallimard/Julliard, 1976. Reprinted as *La Révolution Américaine: 1763-1789*. Édition revue et augmentée ed., Gallimard, 2013.

Kennett, Lee B. *The French Forces in America, 1780-1783*. Greenwood Press, 1977.

Ketchum, Richard M. *Victory at Yorktown: The Campaign That Won the Revolution*. First ed., Henry Holt, 2004.

Lauberdière Louis François Bertrand Dupont d'Aubevoye. *The Road to Yorktown: The French Campaigns in the American Revolution, 1780-1783*. Edited by Norman Desmarais, Savas Beatie, 2020.

Levasseur, Auguste. *Lafayette en Amérique, en 1824 et 1825, Ou, Journal d'Un Voyage Aux États-Unis*. Baudouin, 1829.
    Memoirs of the Marshall Count de Rochambeau. New York Times, 1971.

Marienstras Élise, and Association française d'études américaines, editors. *L'Amérique et la France, Deux Révolutions: [Actes Des Ateliers Histoire Et Politique Du Colloque De Chantilly, Mai 1988]*. Publications De La Sorbonne, 1990.

Marienstras, Elise, and Naomi Wulf. *Révoltes et Révolutions en Amérique*. Atlande, 2005.

McCullough, David G. *1776*. Simon & Schuster, 2005.
Middlekauff, Robert. *The Glorious Cause: The American Revolution, 1763-1789*. 2nd ed., 2nd ed., Oxford University Press, USA, 2007.

Monaque, Rémi. *Une histoire de la Marine de Guerre Française*. Editions Perrin, 2016.

Napier, William Francis Patrick, et al. *Histoire De La Guerre Dans La Peninsule et Dans le Midi de la France Depuis 1807 Jusqu'à 1814*. 8 volumes, Treuttel & Würtz, 1830.

Pichon René Georges, and Claude Fohlen. "*Contribution à l'Étude de la Participation Militaire de la France à la Guerre d'Indépendance des Etats-Unis, 1778-1783.*" S.n, 1976.

Purcell, L. Edward. *Who Was Who in the American Revolution*. Facts on File, 1993.

Rice, Howard C, et al. *The American Campaigns of Rochambeau's Army, 1780, 1781, 1782, 1783*. Princeton University Press, 1972.

Rochambeau, Jean-Baptiste-Donatien de Vimeur, and J.-Charles-J, Luce de Lancival. *Mémoires Militaires, Historiques et Politiques de Rochambeau: Ancien Maréchal de France, et Grand Officier de la Légion D'honneur*. Fain, 1809.

Scott, Samuel F. *From Yorktown to Valmy: The Transformation of the French Army in an Age of Revolution*. University Press of Colorado, 1998.

Shachtman, Tom. *How the French Saved America: Soldiers, Sailors, Diplomats, Louis XVI, and the Success of a Revolution*. First ed., St. Martin's Press, 2017.

United States. National Park Service. *Washington-Rochambeau Revolutionary Route: Resource Study & Environmental Assessment*. U.S. Dept. of the Interior, National Park Service, 2006. https://www.nps.gov/waro/learn/management/upload/ResourceStudyEA_BODY_LO.pdf

Villiers, Patrick. *Le Commerce Colonial Atlantique et la Guerre d'Indépendence des États-Unis d'Amérique, 1778-1783*. Arno Press, 1977.

Wahlen, Auguste. *Nouveau Dictionnaire De La Conversation: ou repertoire universel de toutes les connaissances nécessaires, utiles ou agréables dans la vie sociale, et relatives aux sciences, aux lettres, aux arts, à l'histoire, à la géographie, etc., avec la biographie des principaux personnages, morts et vivants, de tous les pays, sur le plan du conversation's lexicon, par une société de littérateurs, de savants et d'artistes*. Nabu Press, 2012.

Washington, George, and John C Fitzpatrick. *The Writings of George Washington: From the Original Manuscripts Sources 1745-1799*. Government Printing Office, 1938.

Washington, George, et al. *The Papers of George Washington*. University Press of Virginia, 1983.

Wood, Gordon S. *The Radicalism of the American Revolution*. 1st Vintage books ed., Vintage Books, 1993.

Index

abatis, 21, 55, 117, 125, 128
Agenois, 87, 111, 112
Aigrette, 102, 104-106
Albany, NY, 24, 45, 73
Alexandria, VA, 98-101, 103
Alsace, 9
Amelia County, 66
Amsterdam, 9
Annapolis, MD, 3, 88, 99- 104, 106
Arbuthnot, Admiral Marriot, 26
Armonk, NY, 37
Arnold, Benedict, 26, 136
Artillery, 69, 78
Astree, 65
Augusta, GA, 26, 47
baggage, 3, 27, 40, 42, 74, 75, 77, 79, 80, 89, 91, 93, 94, 96, 99, 101, 104, 108, 109, 111
Bald Friar's Ferry, 3, 90-93
Baltimore, MD, 4, 90, 94-99
Barras, Jacques-Melchior Saint-Laurent, Comte de, 46, 63, 68, 76, 100, 102
Battle of... See name of location
Bazley, Mr., 117
Bedford, NY, 28, 32, 37-39
Berthier, Louis Alexandre, 2, 7, 8, 16, 39, 55, 74-76, 79, 91-94, 144
Béville, Pierre François de, 1, 2, 6, 7, 15, 18, 23-26, 29-32, 37-39, 43, 50, 57, 59, 62, 65, 67, 68, 71, 72, 74-78, 80, 82, 85, 87, 89, 91, 92, 94-96, 98, 100, 101, 103, 105-107, 109

bivouac, 18, 54, 75, 78
Bladensburg, MD, 99
Blockhouses, 128
Bolton, CT, 24, 25
Bonaparte, Napoléon, 11, 12
Boston, MA, 8, 65, 67
Bouillé, François Claude Amour, marquis de, 47
Boulogne, 12
Bourbonnais, 34, 48, 51, 64, 78, 79, 95, 112, 113, 117, 158
Brandywine, Battle of, 87
Breakneck, CT, 29, 30
Broglie, Charles-Louis Victor, Prince de, 8
Bronx, NY, 41-43, 45, 52-54, 57, 59, 65, 68, 74
Brune, Guillaume Marie-Anne
Brune, 1st Count Brune, 11
Brunswick, NJ, 83
Burgoyne, John, 41, 73
Bushtown, MD, 3, 90, 93, 94
Cambis, Joseph de
Cambis vicomte de, 106
Camden, Battle of, 136
Cap Français, Haiti, 57, 61, 68
Cape Fear, NC, 86
Cape Henry, VA, 123, 125, 126
Caracas, Venezuela, 138-140
Chandler, John, 30

153

Charles X, 4, 13
Charlestown, frigate, 65
Charlestown, MD, 89
Charlestown, SC, 25, 116
Charon, 121
chasseurs, see also light
    infantry, 21, 22, 31
Chastellux, François-Jean de, 16,
    54, 72, 82, 90, 100, 143, 144
Chesapeake Bay, 87-89, 91,
    96, 105, 106, 110
Chester, PA, 85, 87
Choisy, Claude Gabriel
Marquis de, 109, 111, 119, 121, 122
Clinton, General Henry, 63, 72, 82
Closen, Ludwig, Baron von,
    7, 16, 90, 103, 144
Clove, NJ, 79
College Creek, VA, 107, 108
College Landing, VA, 107, 109
Collot, Georges Henri Victor, 39
communication, 17, 31, 33, 38, 44,
    50, 62, 64, 65, 68, 112, 126, 138
Concorde, frigate, 68, 71
Cornwallis, Sir Charles, 17, 25, 26,
    44, 57-59, 63, 65, 100, 105, 108,
    109, 117, 121, 122, 137, 138
Coromandel, 69
cowboys, 32
Crompond, NY, 32, 33, 37, 73
Croton, NY, 57, 68, 72, 74, 75, 79
Croton River, 57, 74
Cummings Tavern, 92
Custine, Adam Philippe,
Comte de, 88
Damas, Charles-César
d'Antigny, comte de, 54
Danbury Road, 31
d'Autichamp, Antoine-Joseph-
Eulalie de Beaumont, marquis, 111

de Lancey's mill, 53, 54
Deer Creek Church, 93
Delarue, Marie Adelaïde Julie, 9
Delaware River, 7
Delaware, ford of, 85, 86
deserters, 46, 48, 58, 61, 72
Digby, Admiral Robert, 110
Dijon, 11
Diligente, 102
Dismal Swamp, VA, 66, 132, 134, 136
Dobbs Ferry, NY, 50, 51, 53, 56, 64
Dumas de St. Fulcran, 5
Dumas, Mathieu, 1-19, 21, 22, 24,
    26, 32, 55, 64, 91, 93, 98, 103, 107,
    115, 119, 123, 130, 131, 142, 145
Dumas, Guillaume Mathieu, 5
Dumas de St Marcel, 5, 15, 29
Dyckman Bridge, 55
East Hartford, CT, 25-27
East Indies, 69
Eastchester, NY, 52, 64, 68
Eastchester road, 64
École d'Application de Génie, 5
Elizabeth River, 123-125, 137
Elk Ridge Landing, 98
Elkton, MD see Head of Elk
engineers, 7, 110, 119, 122
Farmington, CT, 27, 29
fascines, 21, 119, 120, 128
Ferry Point, VA, 124, 125, 127
Fersen, Hans Axel von, 1, 2, 7,
    16, 40, 71, 75, 104, 140, 145
Fishkill Landing, 33
flag of truce, 63
Fleury, Jean-François Joly de, 63, 76
forage, 27, 43, 44, 46, 58,
    59, 63, 64, 68, 93
Fort George, 53-55
Fort Knyphausen, 40, 55
Fort Laurel, 54

Fort no. 8, 8, 54, 56
Fort Prince Charles, 55
Fort Washington, 40, 50, 53
Frogs Neck see Throggs Neck, NY,
gabions, 21, 119
Gambs, Jean-Daniel de, 64
garrison, 2, 40, 41, 46, 53, 61
Gatinois, 87, 111
Gentille, 102
Georgetown Ferry, 99
Georgetown, VA, 98-102
Gloucester, VA, 109, 111, 119, 121, 122
Grasse, François Joseph Paul Comte de, 47, 51, 58, 61, 64, 68, 71, 86-88, 97, 99, 100, 102, 105, 110, 111
Great Bridge, VA, 124-126, 137
Greene, General Nathanael, 25, 47, 58, 66, 116
grenadiers, 21, 31, 32, 38, 39, 42, 48, 52-54, 59, 64, 68, 74, 75, 88, 99, 108, 109, 111, 113, 117, 140
Guibert, General, 9
Hall, VA, 32, 124-126, 137, 158
Hamburg, Germany, 11, 91
Hamilton, Alexander, 11, 45, 71, 142
Hampton Bay, 106, 124
Hampton Road, 113, 117
Hampton, VA, 106, 118, 124
Harbor Creek, 55
Harlem River, 53-56
Hartford, CT, 24-30
Hartmann, Jacques, 51
Haverstraw, NY, 78, 79
Head of Elk, MD, 3, 82, 85, 86, 88-90, 94, 99
Hermione, frigate, 47, 65
Hessians, 53, 69
Highlands, NY, 33, 79

Hollingsworth, Henry, 85, 86
Hood, Admiral Samuel first Viscount, 97
horse, 4, 18, 28, 39, 42, 51, 54, 82, 88, 93, 115, 122
howitzers, 49, 50, 88, 111
Hudson River, see also North River, 7, 17, 33, 40, 49, 50, 56, 73
Huntington Bay, 46, 48
hussars, 3, 22, 52, 71, 111, 112
Hyder Ali Khan, 69
Iris, 102
Isle of Wight, VA, 103, 132
jaegers, 22
Jamaica, 8, 15
James River, 57, 58, 65, 106-108, 119, 124, 131, 132
Jamestown, VA, 87, 88, 131, 132
Kings Ferry, NY, 50, 72-76, 78, 79
Kingsbridge, NY, 27, 28, 40-43, 50-55, 58, 62, 64, 72
Lambert Crossing, 124
Lameth, Alexandre-Théodore-Victor, comte de, 1, 2, 7, 28, 38, 75, 79, 105
Lauberdière, Louis François Bertrand Dupont d'Aubevoye, comte de, 2, 3, 7, 30, 123, 158
Lauzun, Armand Louis de Gontaut–Biron, Duc de, 38, 40, 41, 88, 111, 120-122
Lauzun's Legion, 11, 12, 28, 38, 39, 41, 42, 48, 51-53, 59, 64, 68, 81, 82, 90-93, 96, 98, 99, 109, 111, 113, 115
Laval, Anne Alexandre Marie Sulpice Joseph de Montmorency, marquis de, 95
Lebanon, CT, 28

155

Legion of Honor, 11, 12
Lents Bridge, 73
Leslie, Alexander, 136
light infantry, see also chasseurs, 5, 22, 31, 32, 38, 39, 42, 48, 51-54, 58, 59, 64, 68, 74, 75, 88, 99, 108, 109, 113, 115, 117
Lincoln, General Benjamin, 41, 42
Little Falls, MD, 94, 95
Lloyd, Mrs. Joanna Leigh, 103, 104
Loménie, François Alexandre Antoine, vicomte de, 64
Long Island Sound, 46, 54, 59, 62-64, 68
Long Island, 28, 41, 46, 54, 63
Louis XVI, 4, 9, 10, 13, 38, 58, 63, 144, 147
Louis XVIII, 4, 13
Lower Ferry, 3, 89, 90, 94
Luzerne, Anne-César de la, 44, 142
Magicienne, frigate, 75
Malabar, 69
Malken Hill, VA, 65
Mamaroneck, NY, 59
Marterici Mr., 140
Mathews, Colonel, 127, 132 Edward (Mathew),
Mauduit, Thomas-Antoine de Mauduit du Plessis, 117
McDonald, Étienne Jacques-Joseph-Alexandre Macdonald, 1st Duke of Taranto,
Mead Mr., 131, 132
Metz, France, 10
Mézières, France, 21
Middletown, CT, 28
militiamen, 100, 111, 115, 120
Millstone River, 83
Moravian, 8
Morris, Robert, Jr., 71

Morrisania, NY, 52-54, 56
Morristown, NJ, 82
Motte Piquet, Count Toussaint-Guillaume Picquet de la Motte, 58, 64
Mullin, (Mullen), William, 87
Nansemond Creek, 132
Nansemond River, 126
Napoléon see Bonaparte,
National Guard, 9, 14
Necker, Jacques, 63, 65, 76
Negro/Negroes, 22, 100, 138-140
Nelson's Quarters, 112
New Rochelle, NY, 63, 64, 68, 73
New York, 7, 14-16, 18, 26, 32, 37, 38, 41-43, 45, 46, 48-52, 54, 56, 58, 59, 61, 63, 65, 69, 71, 79, 80, 110, 144, 145, 146
Newport, Rhode Island, 6, 46, 158
Newtown, CT, 28-32
Ninety-Six, SC, 26, 58
Noailles, Louis-Marie, viscount de, 88
Norfolk, VA, 66, 124, 125, 127, 132, 137
North Castle, NY, 38-40, 42, 59, 65, 72-74
North River, see also Hudson River, 33, 41, 43, 49, 50, 55, 56, 62, 73, 77, 79, 81
North Salem, NY, 4, 38
Norwalk, CT, 38
Octoraro, PA, 90-92
Oxford, CT, 28, 145, 147
Paris, 5, 9-11, 13, 34, 54, 103, 143, 144
Parker, Colonel Josiah, 132
Parsippany, NJ, 82
Patapsco River, 98
Patriot Revolution of 1785–1787, 9
Patuxent River, 105
Pays Mr., 140

Peekskill, NY, 29-31, 33, 41, 73, 77
Pensacola garrison, 61
Philadelphia, PA, 71, 82, 85, 86, 87, 99
Philipsburg, NY, 16, 42, 43, 56, 67, 79
Pigeon Hill, VA, 113
Pines Bridge, NY, 37, 50,
   57, 68, 72, 74, 75
Piney Branch Brook, VA, 98
pirogue, 133
Plainfield, CT, 24
plunder, 58, 62
Pompton Meeting
   House, Plains, River, 81
Pondicherry, 69
Poplar Tree, VA, 117
Porto Cabello, Venezuela, 138, 140
Potomac River, 66, 90, 97,
   99, 100, 102, 105
Prince William, 110
Princeton, NJ, 16, 55, 70, 83, 144, 147
Providence, RI, 7, 14, 16,
   23, 24, 40, 58, 158
Puerto Rico, 8, 138
Puységur, François Jacques
   Chastenet, Marquis de, 6, 24, 72
Quaker, 95
Québec, 65
Rappahannock River, 105
Rations, 50
Rawdon, Francis, Lord, 25, 58, 102
reconnaissance, 5, 7, 29, 30, 42, 43,
   48, 50, 53, 54, 56, 58, 65, 66, 75,
   80, 89, 96, 97, 115, 119, 121, 123
reconnoiter, 9, 27, 32, 38, 41,
   48, 50, 54, 57, 62, 63, 68, 77,
   80, 83, 89, 90, 91, 112, 119
Red Lion Tavern, NJ, 85
Reign of Terror, 10
Renaud, Jean-François, comte
   de Reynaud de Villeverd, 68

Richemond, 102, 106
Ridgebury, CT, 32, 37-39
riflemen, 108, 115
Rochambeau, Donatien-Marie-
   Joseph de Vimeur, vicomte de, 57, 88
Rochambeau, Jean Baptiste
   Donatien de Vimeur Comte de, 6-8,
   16, 18, 26-28, 30, 32, 33, 39, 40, 42,
   44, 46, 50, 54, 55, 57, 63, 70, 71,
   75, 78-80, 82, 87-90, 100, 104, 105,
   107-113, 117, 142, 146, 147, 158
Rodney, Sir George Brydges,
   47, 48, 51, 58
Roebuck, 101
Romulus, 102, 106, 107
Rouen, 9
Royal Deux-Ponts, 7, 79, 80
Ruby, frigate, 101
Rye Neck, NY, 59
Saint Domingue, 6, 8, 57
Sainte-Foy-la-Grande, 15
Saintonge, 34, 35, 40, 64
Saint-Simon, Claude-Anne
   de Rouvroy, marquis de
   Saint-Simon-Montbléru,
   87, 100, 108, 111
Salem Valley, NY, 32
saucissons, 21, 119
Scammell, Alexander, 30, 51, 115, 117
Ségur, Louis Philippe, comte de, 8
Serpent, cutter, 88
Sheldon, Elisha, 28, 37, 38,
   41, 48, 49, 51, 92, 97
Society for the History
   of Protestantism in the
   Dordogne Valley, 15
Society of the Cincinnati, 9
Soissonnais, 34, 35, 112
Somerset Courthouse, NJ, 83
Southington, CT, 29

Spain, 12, 61, 138, 140, 145
Springfield, NJ, 81
Spurrier's Tavern, VA,
Spuyten Duyvil, NY, 53, 55
St. Eustatius, 58, 65
Ste. Lucie, 44, 48
Stone Mrs., 103
Stony Point, NY, 26, 50,
    72, 73, 76, 77, 79
Stratford Road, 31
Suffern, NJ, 79, 80
Suffolk, VA, 125, 126, 132, 136
Sumter, General Thomas, 58
surveyors, 110
Susquehanna River, 3, 7, 89-92, 94
Switzerland, 10
Tallmadge, Major Benjamin, 28
Tappan Sea (Tappan Zee,
    NY), 50, 56, 73
Tarlé, Benoit Joseph de, 29
Tarleton, Colonel Banastre, 122
Tarrytown, NY, 39, 49, 50
Throggs Neck, NY, 54
Titans Hill, NY, 55, 62
Tory/Tories, 22, 30, 32, 37, 97. 100
Touraine, 87, 111
Trebell's Landing, VA,
Trenton, battle of, 67, 83, 85
Tupacamara, 140
Turkey Hill, VA, 52, 68, 71
Upper Salem, NY, 38, 39
Valencia, Venezuela, 138, 140
Valette, Charles-François
    Chevalier Chaudron de la, 64, 92, 94
Varennes, 10
Vauban, Jacques Anne
    Joseph le Prestre, comte de, 1, 2, 7, 40
Vauban, Sébastien Le Prestre de, 21
Verplanck's Point, NY, 72, 73, 76
Vienna, 12

Ville de Paris, 111
Vioménil, Antoine Charles
    du Houx baron de, 8, 27, 39, 40, 74, 75,
    90, 94, 99, 102, 106, 107, 111, 112
volunteers, 38, 111, 112
von Closen see Closen
Wadsworth, Colonel Jeremiah, 27, 91
Warwick Bay, VA, 107
Washington, George, 3, 7, 11, 16,
    28, 30, 33, 40-45, 49, 62, 67, 71,
    76-79, 85, 87-90, 99, 100, 108, 109,
    113, 115, 116, 142, 144, 147, 148
Waterbury, General David, 41, 59
Waterloo, Belgium, 13, 98
Wayne, General Anthony,
    26, 44, 57, 66
West Point, NY, 26, 73, 78, 79
Wethersfield Conference, 7
Wethersfield, CT, 7, 27
Whippany, NJ, 81, 82
White Plains, NY, 30, 32, 39,
    42, 43, 52, 59, 65, 68
White's Tavern,
Willet's Tavern, CT,
William's Bridge, NY,
Williamsburg Creek, 107
Williamsburg, VA, 3, 16, 26, 65, 88, 90,
    100, 104, 107-112, 114, 119, 131, 144
Wilmington, DE, 26, 86-89
Wind Mill Creek, 112
Windham, CT, 24
women, 4, 17, 97, 103
York River, 66
Yorktown, Siege of, 17, 18, 88, 106, 146
Yorktown, VA, 1-3, 7, 15-18, 26,
    32, 37, 38, 41, 46, 47, 60, 64, 66,
    68, 76, 78, 88, 97, 103, 108, 109,
    112, 114-117, 119, 143-147, 158

About the Editor

Norman Desmarais is professor emeritus at Providence College, Providence, Rhode Island, and an active reenactor. He is a member of Le Régiment Bourbonnais, the 2nd Rhode Island Regiment and the Brigade of the American Revolution.

Mr. Desmarais is the author of *The Guide to the American Revolutionary War* series (six volumes about the war on land and seven volumes about the war at sea and overseas), as well as *America's First Ally: France in the American Revolutionary War* and *Washington's Engineer: Louis Duportail and the Creation of an Army Corps*. He is the former editor-in-chief of *The Brigade Dispatch, the Journal of the Brigade of the American Revolution*.

Norm translated the *Gazette Françoise*, the French newspaper published in Newport, Rhode Island by the French fleet that brought the Comte de Rochambeau and 5,800 French troops to America in July 1780. He also translated and annotated Louis-François-Bertrand du Pont d'Aubevoye, comte de Lauberdière's journal, published as The Road to Yorktown: The French Campaigns in the American Revolution, 1780-1783 (Savas Beatie 2021).

Norm also gathered and compiled an extensive, if not exhaustive, collection of Revolutionary War era diaries, journals and memoirs, many of them difficult to obtain. These primary sources include British, Irish, Scottish, German, American, French, Spanish and Swedish perspectives. They have all been digitized in searchable PDF format and can be obtained through RevolutionaryImprints.net.

Mr. Desmarais served as Vice President of Le Foyer Club and the Richelieu Club (which became the Aram Pothier Club), social organizations for the preservation and promotion of the French language and culture. He serves on the Board of Directors of the Boivin Center, University of Massachusetts, Dartmouth.

He was a pioneer in the CD-ROM industry. He set up and managed the first CD-ROM network in Rhode Island and served as Senior Editor of *CD-ROM World*, contributing editor of *Optical Information Systems*, and was the founding editor and editor-in-chief of *Electronic Resources Review*. He is listed in the *International Directory of Distinguished Leadership*, the *Dictionary of International Biography*, *Who's Who of Information Technology*, *2000 Outstanding Intellectuals of the 20th Century*, and *Marquis Who's Who*.

Norm was inducted into the American French Genealogical Society French-Canadian Hall of Fame in 2015 and received the Albert Nelson Marquis Lifetime Achievement Award in 2019 and 2020.

Other Books by Norman Desmarais

Washington's Engineer: Louis Duportail and the Creation of an Army Corps. Lanham MD: Prometheus Books, 2021.

Lauberdière, Louis François Bertrand Dupont d'Aubevoye. *The Road to Yorktown : The French Campaigns in the American Revolution, 1780-1783.* Translated and edited by Norman Desmarais, Savas Beatie, 2020.

America's First Ally: France in the Revolutionary War. Philadelphia & Oxford: Casemate, 2019.

The Guide to the American Revolutionary War in Canada and New England: Battles, Raids, and Skirmishes. Ithaca, NY: BUSCA, 2009.

The Guide to the American Revolutionary War in New York: Battles, Raids, and Skirmishes. Ithaca, NY: BUSCA, 2010.

The Guide to the American Revolutionary War in New Jersey: Battles, Raids, and Skirmishes. Ithaca, NY: BUSCA, 2011.

The Guide to the American Revolutionary War in Pennsylvania, Delaware, Maryland, Virginia and North Carolina: Battles, Raids, and Skirmishes. Ithaca, NY: BUSCA, 2012.

The Guide to the American Revolutionary War in South Carolina: Battles, Raids, and Skirmishes. Ithaca, NY: BUSCA, 2012.

The Guide to the American Revolutionary War in the Deep South and on the Frontier: Battles, Raids, and Skirmishes. Ithaca, NY: BUSCA, 2013.

The Guide to the American Revolutionary War at Sea. [s.l.]: Revolutionary Imprints, 2016.

Raids at Narragansett in *Shoreline: selected short fiction, non-fiction, poetry & prose from The Association of Rhode Island Authors.* Glocester, RI: Stillwater River Publications, 2016. pp. 39-42.

Mr. Desmarais has also written many articles on the Revolutionary War for the *Journal of the American Revolution* (allthingsliberty.com), the *Online Journal of Rhode Island History* (smallstatebighistory.com) and *The Brigade Dispatch, the Journal of the Brigade of the American Revolution.*